Note to the Reader

This book is intended to be used for informational purposes only and is not meant to replace the advice of your individual physician. Readers are advised to consult a trained medical professional before acting on any of the information in this book. The author accepts no liability for the outcome of any decisions or actions prompted by information presented here. The author encourages you to read this book, find in it empowerment, reassurance, and a little humor, and to use what you've learned to have informed and intelligent discussions with your obstetrician and other medical professionals.

Please be aware that medical knowledge is constantly expanding. New research and the constant flow of information may invalidate some of the data presented here and new knowledge may alter your own physician's advice. Read and enjoy this book and your journey, but always discuss your concerns and questions with your physician.

Contents

Acknowledgments

After searching during my own pregnancy for a book that would ease my fears, make me laugh, and provide information, I can't believe I'm now the author of just the book I had needed. So much has gone into this adventure, and I am thankful to all those who have made it happen.

To my parents, Don and Carol McClintock: In a world of uncertainty, you have loved me unconditionally and been my biggest supporters. You have taught me most of what I know and still believe about life—that family is always first, that success is what one makes of it, and that from him (or her) to whom much is given much will be expected. I can only hope that in my life as your child I continue to live up to your expectations and to carry forward your ideas to my own children. I love you more than I can say and am so grateful for all the experiences that have brought us as a family to this time. I wouldn't have changed a thing.

To my one true love, Benjamin Franklin: You remain my stalwart companion and truest friend, my lover, my husband, and the most incredible father to our little ones I could have hoped to find. Thank you for your kindness, your patience through this process, and your love for the twins and me. I am a blessed woman to have married so well. And I know that someday Paris awaits—for real this time!

To my brother, Matt, and his family, and to all my family far and wide: Thanks for giving me the gift of laughter, for loving me through the hard times and rejoicing with me through the good times. I still recall road trips taken, games played, and stories told when I need a pick-me-up after sad or stressful days. The unique blessing that is our family is one I wish all people could experience and one I wish to see preserved for future generations of our children. Stay close.

Many people contributed to my becoming what I've become as a doctor. I will forever be grateful to my uncle, Tom Snyder, M.D., who married Mom's baby sister and promptly took an eight-year-old girl under his wing and nurtured her desire to be a doctor. He even helped me deliver the first baby I'd ever seen born. Thank you for the pep talks, the study sessions, and the hospital rounds. Thank you most of all for your unflagging belief in my dream. The love you bear your patients and the love they show you in return were—and are—my motivation and example of what makes being a doctor a true honor. I mentor high schoolers and medical students alike in the hope of giving them the encouragement I received from you.

To the late Jim Hurley, Ph.D.: I'm sorry I never wrote a book that would be in your line of interest, but I thank you for demanding the best from me and for being my friend. To Jim Barrett, M.D., and Ken Smith, M.D.: Thank you for mentoring me and for your continued friendship. You two saw me through hell and back. I hope to do you proud. To John Stanley, M.D., and Jeff Osburn, M.D.: You taught me much of what I think I know about obstetrics, and then turned that training on me in short order. Thanks forever for the two healthy babies I have and for the care you showed us all.

To all at the University of Oklahoma Family Medicine Residency Program: Thanks for giving me a first-class education, supporting me through some rough waters, and celebrating with me when it all worked out well. Special thanks are due to Bev Finley, the best "den mother" a group of punk kids with degrees could have; thanks for keeping me in line. Also to John Zubialde, M.D.: Thanks for not flunking me when you could have and for those fateful words: "I don't even care if you get married in Eureka as long as you go to the conference." To Steve Crawford, M.D., and Jim Brand, M.D.: Thanks for the champagne, first dance, and first kiss. To Linda Crawford: Thanks for helping me crash that other wedding reception! To Chenedra, Kelly, and Miss Cynthia: Thanks for being there for me and for giving all those shots to my kids—I'll never see the Spice Girls the same way! To my partners and the staff of the Oklahoma City Clinic: Thanks for your support during my pregnancy, motherhood, and the craziness of "the book thing."

I have learned so much about publishing in the last two years, and I've been enthralled the whole time. As a compulsive neophyte I simply did exactly what the books say to do to get published, and I was fortunate to find a first-class agent right off the bat. To Jessica Faust: I am ever grateful that you saw in me what I thought I had as a writer and that you had the patience to take me on. I hope this book is everything you saw in that first query letter and that it does well enough to encourage you to take on such a challenge again.

My first editor, Marian Lizzi, was patient and kind to me in every conversation we had, and I thank her for opening the door to such a prestigious house. Marian, I do hope you find stunning success in your next venture! To Sheila Oakes, my editor: You could easily have chosen to kill a book by an unknown author during the transition and shortened your "to do" list in the process, but you chose to finish the project. I thank you so much for seeing the potential in a book you did not select and for guiding me through this mysterious world. I am looking forward with giddy anticipation to each new step. To Julie Mente: Thanks for being the glue that held this together! And to Courtney Fischer, my St. Martin's publicist: Thanks in advance for your hard work letting the world know this book exists.

And, finally, to you who bought this book: Congratulations on expecting multiples, and thanks for having faith that I will do what I promised—give you enough information to be empowered yet enough humor to relax just a little and enjoy the experience. I hope you find in here exactly the help you were seeking. *Bonne chance!*

Introduction

I love being a family physician. I have wanted to be a doctor since I was six years old. I never, ever wanted to be anything else. My parents, bless their souls, took me seriously, and provided guidance and constant encouragement. They even bought me a *Gray's Anatomy* for Christmas when I was eleven. The only other thing I ever thought I was good at was teaching, and *doctor* means "teacher" in Greek. Little did I know that my professional training and the experiences of my personal life would converge to create my desire to educate others about multiple pregnancy.

I had initially wanted to be a pediatrician because I loved my own, Dr. R. K. Mohan. Bless his heart, I never understood a word he said in his Pakistani accent, but I always knew he loved me—right up until the day he told my mommy I had to start seeing a "grown-up's" doctor.

In medical school I fell in love with delivering babies. My first-ever time seeing a delivery was in the summer before my first year of medical school when I visited my uncle in rural Oklahoma. Dr. Tom Snyder had married my mom's baby sister when I was eight, and he always encouraged me to follow him into medicine. That first delivery—seeing a miracle in the flesh—hooked me for life.

I soon discovered that pediatricians don't deliver babies. I later discovered that obstetricians don't get to keep the babies they deliver. My uncle's influence surfaced again one weekend as I followed him on rounds at the hospital. He sat at the bedside of an elderly woman and touched her shoulder, and the look of love and gratitude in her eyes, demented though she was, spoke volumes about the relationship a family doctor has with his patients. I determined then and there that I would one day be a family physician who delivers babies.

I took great pains to do extra study in obstetrics during medical school and residency, and sought opportunities to care for—and deliver—as many babies as I could. I aligned myself with the OB residents and the high-risk OB doctors, and began developing relationships with those who could teach me skills in cesarean section and other obstetric procedures.

I cared for my first set of twins, born at twenty-six weeks to a seventeen-year-old single mom, on the Newborn Nursery rotation of my intern year, and saw them grow into healthy two-year-olds by the time I left for private practice. I miss those boys, and somehow the wonder of their existence never left my heart.

While becoming a family doctor who delivers babies and still caring for those twins, I soon found myself in love. My life and my desire to educate others would be forever changed.

I am especially fond of the story of my husband's and my romance. We met at church, kissed under the Eiffel Tower, eloped to Eureka Springs, and honeymooned in England. We had known each other only four months when we married and delayed the honeymoon for almost a year. By the time we went "on holiday," we had begun to hope for a child to complete the picture. On the last day of our honeymoon, after driving over nine hundred miles chasing kings and queens through England's history and reveling in the beauty of her landscapes and gardens, before our journey home, we rested in a little town in Kent. We soon learned we had brought home a special British import. I was pregnant.

We began this newest journey by seeing my dear friend Jim Barrett, a doctor who had been responsible for a large part of my learning and who had been my adviser in residency. He and I had noticed my elevated blood pressure but attributed it to the hormonal shift of pregnancy as well as to family history. My staff had begun teasing me about how big my belly had grown, but I laughed it off as my overwhelming desire to be and to look pregnant. Jim would hear the baby on the left side of my body, and I would hear the baby on the right. My husband, Ben, and I laughed at how quickly such a small creature could move about in such a large space. Everything I had ever learned about delivering babies disappeared in a haze of denial . . . but not for long.

Ben and I traveled to California to see family during my seventeenth week of pregnancy. I marveled at the feeling I had of a golf ball rolling in my bladder and thought it was much too early to feel the baby move, especially in a first pregnancy. My family expressed astonishment that I was larger than my cousin who was in her twentieth week.

We came home the following week, and I went for my ultrasound. Normally doctors wait until the second trimester for this in a "low-risk" pregnancy because the baby's features will be large enough to detect many problems and because the insurance usually pays for only one ultrasound—plus, after seventeen or eighteen weeks, it is easier to tell if the baby is a boy or a girl. My ultrasound showed not one but two babies, a boy *and* a girl, happily wriggling in my aching belly. I was having twins. No longer would this be a routine pregnancy for me. Although I deliver babies for a living, despite my extra learning and experience, I was now in the same boat as every other new mom: anxiously awaiting the reassurance of her doctor, fearing the possible dangers I knew might lie ahead, and desperately seeking the information that would empower me to prepare for uncertainty.

I read voraciously—medical textbooks, journal articles, anything I could find. I discovered, unfortunately, that too much knowledge can be dangerous. I encountered more horror stories than hope and found that I became more concerned rather than calmed. I sought reassurance in the pregnancy section of the bookstore but found more lists of complications to expect and little humor or personal sharing.

I wanted a friend with whom I could share my fears. I wanted to once again anticipate the joy of my pregnancy. I began to keep a journal to organize and contain my thoughts, to confront my fears, to remember questions I had for my doctors, and to record the journey for my babies and communicate to them later the hopes and dreams I had for them. That journal has evolved into this book, and through it I hope you will find guidance to weather the uncertainty of multiple childbirth and emerge inspired to see humor and blessing and promise in this most special of events.

PART 1

The Big Surprise and What to Do About It

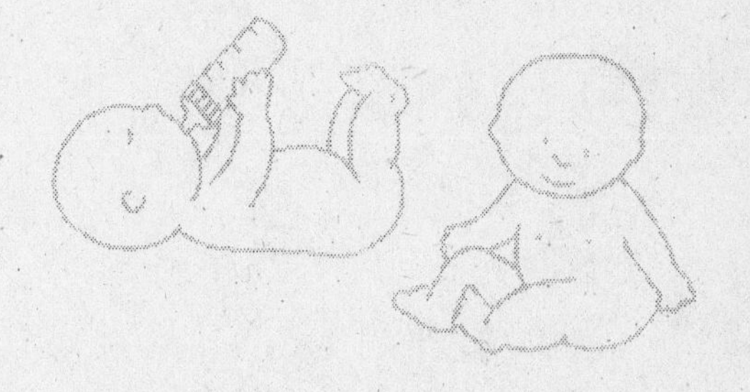

One

"You Knew You Were Having Twins, Right?"

Wot in hell have I done to deserve all these kittens?

–Don Marquis, *Mehitabel and Her Kittens* in *Archy and Mehitabel*

Thursday, November 9, 2000

Yesterday I found out I was pregnant with twins. My husband and I had gone for the routine ultrasound and had waited until I was eighteen weeks along so we could find out the sex of the baby.

I lay on the table and the tech put the goo on my belly. You know the stuff—not quite slime, not yet lotion. I'd always been convinced that some company decided that making conductive gel feel too much like a pleasant spa treatment would make it feel less like an actual diagnostic tool.

I already had the discomfort of a full bladder, and now this lady was pushing the probe right on top of it all. I felt like I was riding in a jeep over giant boulders wearing a too tight seat belt while trying not to pee on myself. But I was anxious to see the child we had made in England, and up until those first words out of the tech's mouth—"You knew you were having twins, right?"—I thought I could handle it.

Some strange picture popped up on the screen, and I quickly recognized it for what it was—the abdomen and the head of a baby, side by side. I knew one baby couldn't make this picture. I was convinced that someone must have put the tech up to this. I had many friends in this hospital. Which one did this?

Then she moved the picture, and I saw two hearts, side by side. Twins!

I went completely numb. Ben, my husband, now says he felt all the blood leave his body. Then, partly recovered, he noticed that I was pale and hyperventilating. "Honey, are you okay?" he asked as he squeezed my hand. "Honey, you're not breathing. You've got to breathe."

"I am breathing," I insisted. I focused on the screen as the picture developed, fully switching into my "doctor mode," as my family calls my coping mechanism. Two sacs, two placentas (good, no twin transfusion—maybe), closed spinal cords (no spina bifida—maybe), intact hearts. The larger picture soon emerged in my mind: Side by side in separate sacs with the membrane between them running from the top of my uterus to the bottom, and . . . they're perfect. A boy and a girl, we think, with two arms and two legs each, normal bones and hearts, and just the right size for their age.

I began laughing for fear I'd cry.

Whether multiple pregnancy is fortune's touch or the result of an arduous journey through the infertility clinics of the world, it is inevitably somewhat of a shock to most of us. While many who read this book may have known sooner than others that they would be carrying multiples, their uncertainty will likely be no less acute. You will undoubtedly have many of the fears and insecurities I had when first embarking on this adventure.

I want you to know that you've joined a sisterhood (and an amazingly strong fraternity for you dads) that is largely invisible to the world of "one kid at a time" families. You will be embraced (and accosted) with more stories than the average expectant mom. You will receive the stares and comments of those uneducated souls who think you're just plain fat. You will hear horror stories of terrible outcomes and predictions of the end of your social life from those who had only one at a time. I have been told, "Honey, you really need to watch what you're eating. Baby doesn't need all that," and "Just wait until they're six months old. You won't be able to go anywhere." Be kind in your thoughts toward these people; they haven't the slightest clue what you're going through. Ignore the ignorant. They mean well when they're not trying too hard to be clever. My response has typically been to ask them in feigned earnestness how old their twins are. It usually stops the intrusion.

Embrace the parents who have been where you are. They know the truth. Parents of multiples have had the fears you've had, and they've survived. From parents of multiples I have heard only reassurances. Strangers, friends, or patients, they remind me so often what a blessing their twins or triplets are and how they have weathered hardships and come out stronger. Ours, and now yours, is a survivors' club, forever changed by what we have endured and strengthened by new priorities, renewed patience, and a learned behavior of expecting the unexpected.

So, what is a multiple pregnancy, how rare is it really, and how does a couple survive it with their sanity and relationship intact? First, you need to arm yourself with some facts. Then, you need to assemble the team of experts you can trust to guide you the rest of the way through. With luck, patience, and learned skills you can soon begin to deal with stress and with the unexpected conditions of an experience completely out of control.

Definitions

Get ready for the two most common questions you will hear at home, at work, at the grocery store, at church, or at the mall: "Ooh, are they *twins?*" (in the first two years of life I think the answer should be "duh") soon to be followed by "Are they *identical?*" You may also hear my favorite query: "Are they *natural* twins [triplets, and so on], or did you go through fertility treatment?" For some reason the intrusion on one's privacy when one has multiples doesn't end with pregnancy, as it blessedly does for those with a singleton pregnancy.

> Ladies, if your husband is anything like mine, he will undoubtedly take this opportunity to pride himself on his skill at having impregnated you twice or more at one go. Ben was said to have returned to work after the first ultrasound bragging that he had been "shooting from both barrels" the night I conceived. I think it's compensation for their suppressed desire to turn tail and run in the opposite direction from the diagnosis.

Whether you like it or not, you will be fodder for the public's perceived "right to know" for some time. Whether you answer them or not (especially about the fertility treatments), you should be familiar with the terms used when referring to your pregnancy and babies.

By definition, a multiple pregnancy is one in which either more than one egg was fertilized or the fertilized egg split early in its development. The babies produced in a multiple pregnancy are defined in such a way as to clarify the source of multiplication and to help doctors identify potential problems as early as possible. Many of the following definitions are those pertaining to twins. Your doctor can help you with definitions for your pregnancy if you are having more than two babies.

Those babies produced from more than one egg are called *fraternal* twins, triplets, and so on. The medical term for them is *dizygotic* (two eggs) if they are twins. These babies by definition are as similar as any other siblings and will each have her own sac of amniotic fluid and her own placenta. Dizygotic twins will have their own potential complications but will be spared others (discussed in other sections and in the Rapid Reference Guides in chapters 14 and 15). By luck of the draw, these multiples can be any combination of boys and girls.

Babies who are the result of a single fertilized egg splitting are called *monozygotic* (one egg). They share an identical set of genetic material and are of the same sex. They have the potential to look exactly alike, although not all do because of the different ways in which our genetic material can express itself. These eggs split at different stages of development, during which time the parts essential to support life inside the uterus (placenta, fluid, protective sac [chorion], and umbilical cord) are forming. Because of this difference, these babies can live life inside

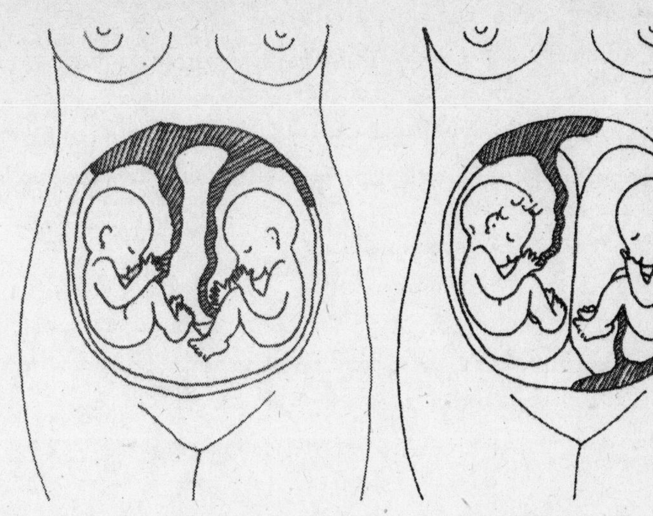

Monoamniotic/monochorionic twins with one placenta

Diamnionic/monochorionic twins with separate placentas

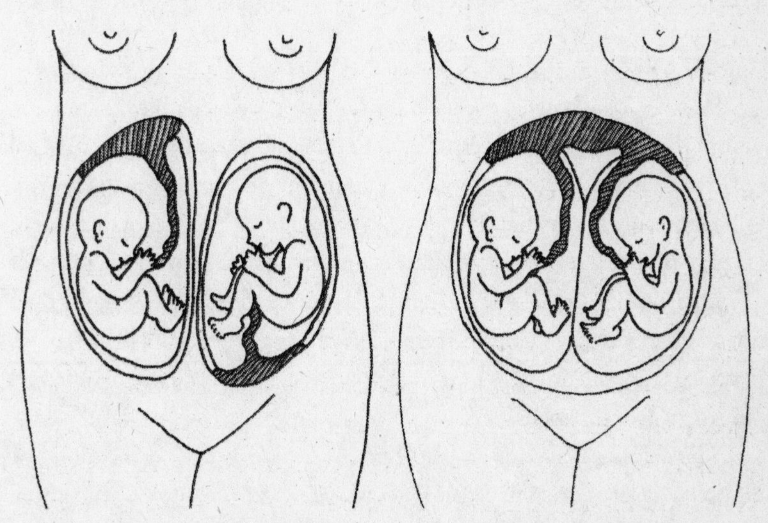

Diamnionic/dichorionic twins with separate placentas

Diamnionic/monochorionic twins with one placenta (fused placenta)

their moms in a variety of conditions. If the egg splits within the first three days, each child will have his own amniotic sac and placenta and live a completely separate life in the womb. They are known as *diamnionic/dichorionic* if they are twins, and frequently have the same promise and potential problems as fraternal (*dizygotic*) multiples. If the egg splits after certain components of fetal life have formed, the babies can share the placenta or sac or both (known as *monoamniotic/monochorionic*). Those eggs that wait too late to split (around days thirteen to fifteen) give rise to conjoined, or Siamese, twins. Very rarely do eggs splitting at this stage result in more than two babies.

> Twins do tend to run in families. The likelihood of having twins resulting from one egg (monozygotic) can be inherited from our mothers, and the likelihood of having twins from two eggs (dizygotic) can be inherited from either parent. The odds of having twins is 1.7 times normal for those whose sisters have had twins, and 2.5 times normal for those who are the children of a twin mother.

Statistics

In 2002, the last year for which statistics are available, there were more than 4 million live births to women of all ages. Just over 125,000 of these births, or 3.1 percent, were to moms of twins, and almost two in a thousand pregnancies resulted in the birth of triplets, quadruplets, or more babies. This represents a continued increase in the number of women having twins and a slight decrease in those having more than two babies per pregnancy. Overall, the chance of having twins has increased from one in eighty (according to a 1993 textbook I have) to one in thirty-two pregnancies!

The chance of having multiple births increases with older mothers, those who used assistive technologies (Clomid, in vitro fertilization, and so on; see the discussion below), and with mothers of African-American heritage, followed by non-Hispanic black women and Caucasian women. If you are a new member of this sisterhood, you remain unusual to the rest of the world, but you will probably see another parent of multiples at the mall about every other time you go shopping with yours.

The incidence or number of multiple pregnancies each year has risen dramatically since 1990, with the number of moms having twins increasing 30 to 80 percent, depending on race; the number having triplets increasing over 400 percent; quads, more than 1100 percent; and quints or more, over 500 percent. The greatest increase has been seen among older women (more than forty years old). From 2001 to 2002 the number of twin births to women over forty increased 10 percent.

A study published in 2000 showed that 43 percent of multiple births were the result of "assistive reproductive technologies," such as in vitro fertilization in which multiple embryos are created by the union of sperm and egg in a laboratory and then placed inside the mother to increase the chance of a successful pregnancy. Forty percent of multiple births were due to the use of medications such as Clomid (clomiphene), designed to stimulate the ovaries to make eggs, or to intrauterine insemination, in which the sperm is placed directly inside the woman in a doctor's office. The use of these technologies is reflected in the higher incidence of twins in women over forty-five. The number of women in this age group who had babies in the years 1990 to 2002 increased from 39 to 991 per year, and the risk of each pregnancy resulting in twins increased from 1 in 43 to 1 in 5.5! The controversy that surrounds the use of these technologies can result in an emotional strain on couples already desperate to have a child, and it is not my primary focus in writing this book. Suffice it to say that there are simply a lot more of us having a lot more babies at once than our mothers had. In fact, 18 percent of triplets or more are conceived naturally!

Unfortunately, the risk of having problems in your pregnancy is higher than for your friends who are expecting one child, but for the most part they are manageable or even preventable with early prenatal care and frequent monitoring. These will be discussed in more detail later in the book, but I include the most common and most obvious here because I know my mind was racing with terrors long before I went in search of information. What is most likely to happen, and why do you need to be certain you have a concerned and skilled team of health care professionals behind you in your quest for a healthy outcome?

First, multiple pregnancy carries with it a higher risk of preterm labor and low birth weight babies. Twins have a greater than fifty-fifty chance of being "low birth weight" (born weighing less than 5 pounds 5 ounces) and a 10 percent chance of being "very low birth weight" (weighing less than 3 pounds 4 ounces). The risk for triplets is 94 and 38 percent, respectively. Nearly 100 percent of pregnancies with more than three babies result in prematurity and low birth weight. This makes sense when you consider that most of us were built with a uterus designed to carry only about 15 pounds' worth of baby plus other stuff (fluid, placenta, and so on).

Start considering now how you can arrange it if your doctor someday suddenly says that hospitalization, bed rest, reduced work hours, or reduced workload are necessary. Start the nursery now or find someone who can do it for you. Get ready for that hair-raising event known as "telling the boss," to be discussed later.

As a result of the increase in early delivery and low birth weight, you may find yourself in the Neonatal Intensive Care Unit (NICU) caring for your newborns. This can be a stressful experience for new parents, whether first-timers or those with other children at home. Early preparation can help you be more comfortable with the staff and doctors who will care for your precious ones, and allow for financial stability during what may become a prolonged period of adjustment.

Dealing With It All

November 9, 2000

So many worries. We figured we could do the "one kid, two jobs" thing, but we don't know anyone with twins where mom doesn't stay home. My brother's wife had wanted to be our nanny, but how could she agree to twins when she has a little one still at home? What will I do with preeclampsia, preterm labor, bed rest, labor, and delivery (an epidural is definitely an option now), NICU, amniocentesis, and four hundred more of these lovely ultrasounds? How can I still see patients and build a practice? How in the world am I supposed to breast-feed twins? How can I get them on a schedule so I have time to sleep?

All I can say is that God must have a wonderful sense of humor. He must have decided that Ben and I were having way too much fun and that I was just a bit cocky. Well now, I'm challenged.

We all have our own ways of dealing with stress, and each method can be either healthy or harmful. For those of you who would otherwise resort to smoking or drinking, let me be the first to tell you that neither is a good way to deal with pregnancy. In fact, many of us doctor types think it's downright bad for your babies' health. If you do smoke or drink alcohol, stop now. If you smoke, never start again—it was a bad idea to begin with.

For those of you who would love nothing better than a five-mile run, I'm afraid your doctor may not allow it in a multiple pregnancy. To those who eat until they can eat no more to combat stress, I see where you're coming from—just don't overdo it. Some of the complications of multiple birth to be discussed later require careful adherence to a healthy diet, and remember that any unnecessary weight you put on is weight you have to try to lose later. The "baby weight" excuse lasts only so long, even with a twin (or more) pregnancy.

Handling the Shock

A multiple pregnancy is a voyage into the unknown, and that can be frightening. In fact, for those who, like me, are compulsive control freaks, it can be downright maddening. Allow yourself to be a little scared for now if you need to be. Things will get better later, and a tincture of time is a balm for many worries. If you have a need for control, recognize first that you need to work on controlling your stress.

Stress hormones increase the risk of many of the problems you may already fear, including high blood pressure, preterm labor, and other complications. Letting fear and stress get the better of you will only make the situation worse.

Try journaling your thoughts. I kept a journal by my bedside, and after years of failed attempts to keep one faithfully, I found that the wakeful hours of the night and early morning that come with the incessant kicking, heartburn, and general sensation of a bowling ball in my belly made for ideal times to write. My husband, bless his soul, was fast asleep, and there is still nothing good on television late at night, even with thousands of channels. When rereading those thoughts and fears while writing this book, almost two years after my babies' birth, I realized how much of the pain, comfort, fear, pure joy, and sheer expectation I had forgotten. At the time it had been helpful for keeping track of what my doctors had told us and for noting questions to be asked at follow-up visits. Now it is a connection to that time for my husband, my children, and me, free from the distortions of distant memory. The anecdotes in each chapter of this book are synopses of those early raw thoughts.

Don't be concerned about your writing skills if you journal. Even the most disjointed or poorly spelled or vaguely worded thoughts will remind you years later of the exact feelings you had. Write down your fears to objectify and control them. Write your hopes to share with your children later. Write down your prayers and watch how they change over time. Write about the changes your body goes through. Write about your joys. Write about your discomforts. Write about other people's reactions to your pregnancy and whether they amused, frustrated, or frightened you. Write down your "to do" lists and when you finished them. Note how long it took to accomplish them in your new reality.

Invite your babies' father to write in the journal. One of the most poignant and memorable passages in mine is a four-page summary my husband wrote of a hospital stay for an illness I had, two days of which I don't remember. I had a high fever and abdominal pain, and went into preterm labor. My doctors later decided it was just a viral illness made worse by my pregnant condition, but during the time it was happening, they were worried enough about an internal infection to consider an amniocentesis, in which a needle is placed inside the uterus and fluid removed to test for problems. In the journal Ben described with tearfulness his love for me and our twins, as yet unborn, and the fear he felt when facing the outcome of my illness. It stands now as a testament to the love we hope our children will take with them into the world and as a message to them of how to love one's spouse.

If you are more comfortable with scrapbooking, start now. You will have more ultrasound pictures, more pieces of paper to save, and more factoids to record than you ever imagined. Buy a good-quality scrapbook and record the day you found out you were pregnant, the day you found out how many babies you were to have, each month of pregnancy, how you came to name each child, and what the weather was like when you went into the hospital to deliver them. Take photographs of yourself at each stage of pregnancy—your burgeoning belly, your swollen feet, your glossy hair. Save their hospital bands, their newborn footprints, their bassinet name cards. Even consider saving the hospital bill; you'll probably want to use it as leverage when they want those new cars on their sixteenth birthdays. Consider keeping a scrapbook for the pregnancy and first year of life for each child, remembering that each is his or her own person. By the time you deliver, you will have begun your memory albums and spent a few hours in pleasurable activities related to the pregnancy that might otherwise have found you consumed with your worries. Remember that this *is* your pregnancy, and it is a time in your life well worth vivid remembrance.

Exercise has long been known to be a healthy adaptation to stress. In most people, moderate exercise lowers blood pressure, raises good cholesterol, increases energy levels, and decreases the risk of heart attack. Exercise decreases stress and has been shown to help in problem-solving efforts. It prevents obesity and prepares you for the habit of spending time on yourself each day when the children are born. Strenuous exercise has even more benefits—in a nonpregnant woman. I'll discuss your goals for returning to fitness a little later. Meanwhile, if your constantly shifting puppy sack of a belly hasn't reminded you, you are pregnant with multiples and need different guidance.

For those of you who are accustomed to regular exercise, ask your doctor what you can safely do. While moderate exercise in most pregnant women can increase birth weight and decrease delivery time as well as some complications of pregnancy, women pregnant with multiple babies are at risk for hypertension and preterm labor. Exercises that can safely be done in most pregnancies will be discussed in chapters 3 and 4.

Be sure you continue to seek the joy in the everyday living of life as you anticipate the needs of the future. Continue to work if it gives you comfort or fulfillment, as long as your physician allows it. Maintain your social life for as long as you can tolerate it and as long as your health holds out. Make it a priority to pause every day for one hour for yourself and your spouse. If you have other children, put them to bed or to do their homework or to play while you reconnect with a warm bath or quiet time. Let the world know that you are special during this time and that you need extra care.

If you are having difficulty squelching the stress and finding the quiet and joyful moments of your pregnancy, consider the possibility of seeking counseling. The two faces of pregnancy are that everyone else expects you to be continuously giddy and glowing while you may be feeling just the opposite. Signs of abnormal feelings are persistent uncontrollable anxiety or feelings of sadness, especially when accompanied by poor sleep, an inability to find the joy in once-pleasurable activities, and disruption in close relationships because of the feelings. True clinical depression or anxiety attacks can put your pregnancy at risk. If this persists for long, let your doctor know and ask for a referral to a counselor or seek one in your community.

Renew your acquaintances with dear friends and loved ones near you. Be unafraid to reach out around you and let it be known that you will need help. You *will need help* when your babies are born. If you belong to a family of faith, reach out to the ministers of your congregation, the women's groups, and the benevolence ministries. This is one time in your life when you will need to learn to ask unashamedly for help. Even those of us who are by nature self-sufficient need assistance during the transition from expectant couple to accomplished parents. Assembling your volunteer workforce will serve you well on the day you tire of the week you spent without a shower, the month you've had with no sleep, or the cold that knocks you down and prevents you from giving your babies the full attention they need. Whether you need a nap, a warm meal, another diaper run to the store, a date for yourself and your husband, or a round-the-clock shift for the feeding, diapering, and care of quadruplets, you will serve yourself well by being prepared now.

Many of us fear asking for others to take from their own lives to assist us in ours. Don't. Friends and loved ones are often waiting to hear what you need and are ready to jump on the bandwagon. Asking in advance allows time for them to work out their own schedules and lets them avoid the assumption that you must be doing just fine without them.

Take advantage of the friendships and support that can be obtained by connecting with other parents of multiples. Many Mothers of Multiples (MOM) or similar groups exist across the country and have been established to share thoughts, concerns, common experiences, and even hand-me-downs. The Resources section in the back of the book contains names of groups to contact in your area and Web sites with chat rooms to surf and perhaps to join.

As you work to combat the extra measure of worry that can accompany this unfamiliar kind of pregnancy, you also need to focus on assembling your medical team and preparing for the logistic and financial aspects of your new life. By doing so as early as possible, you can prevent or delay many of the problems you are concerned about.

"I got more children than I can rightly take care of, but I ain't got more than I can love." —Ossie Guffy

Famous Parents of Multiples

Madeleine Albright
Muhammad Ali
Meredith Baxter
Corbin Bernsen
Debby Boone
President and Mrs. George W. Bush
Beverly D'Angelo (with Al Pacino)
Robert De Niro
Milos Forman
Michael J. Fox (with Tracy Pollan)
Mel Gibson
Peri Gilpin
Marcia Gay Harden
Ron Howard
Joseph Kennedy
Emeril Lagasse
Joan Lunden
Martie Maguire (of the Dixie Chicks)
Cathy Moriarty
Soledad O'Brien
Jane Pauley (with Gary Trudeau)
Holly Robinson Peete
Lou Diamond Phillips
Patricia Richardson
Julia Roberts
Kenny Rogers
Ray Romano
Jane Seymour (with James Keach)

Cybill Shepherd
Donald Sutherland (Kiefer and his sister)
James Taylor
Niki Taylor
Cheryl Tiegs
Denzel Washington
Mary Alice Williams

Two

Assembling the Team

November 21, 2000

Saw Jeff Osburn today. I've known him since medical school (he taught my first lesson in obstetrics), and I was able to deliver my niece with his help. He's a soft-spoken and very nice man, and I think he's an excellent doctor. He confirmed my fears for the most part—I am higher risk for preeclampsia, preterm labor, and the like, and my blood pressure is already above the safe zone. I got lab and a jug for my first-ever 24-hour urine collection—joy. . . . I am to start taking Aldomet for the blood pressure tonight.

December 12, 2000

Saw Dr. John Stanley today. He formerly trained in family medicine and then went into ob-gyn and perinatology (high-risk OB). Jeff had sent me for a "level-II ultrasound" to assess the babies' growth and development. Dr. Stanley did see mild enlargement of part of the kidneys in each child, but he didn't think much of it for now.

It has been so reassuring to have the care I've received.

Medical Providers

Expectant parents want the best possible care for their unborn children. The problem is that the world of doctors and medicine often feels mysterious and confusing. How do loving parents-to-be find the right physicians who will care for our pregnancy and our children in a way that will help us with the stress of the unknown?

For many of you this pregnancy has come as a surprise. You may be at the greatest disadvantage in this search because you have not been deeply involved with the medical world. By definition, however, you have a high-risk pregnancy, and although you may have a family doctor, pediatrician, or ob-gyn, you will need other doctors, too. I was fortunate to have been a part of this community already and knew who I wanted to care for me.

Primary Care Obstetrician

Your primary physician will be the man or woman who monitors your pregnancy and delivers your babies. You will contact this person as soon as you know you are pregnant because, of course, you will want that "official" test to prove to your partner that you have reason to be so cranky all of a sudden. The two types of physicians who perform most prenatal care are obstetrician/gynecologists and family physicians. Other, nonphysician practitioners such as nurse midwives deliver babies as well, but I recommend staying with a physician for a multiple pregnancy. A family medicine physician specializes in care "from cradle to grave," and some (like me) include obstetrics as part of their practice. Family physicians have been through four years of medical school and then receive three years more of specialty training, after which they must pass board examinations to become board certified.

> Regardless of the doctor's specialty, be sure your doctor is board certified. This means that the physician has proved to a national certifying body by taking tests that she is qualified to call herself a certain type of doctor, whether it be surgeon, internal medicine physician, or dermatologist.

While there are a few family physicians who have done extra training to certify them to perform so-called high-risk deliveries, many defer to ob-gyn colleagues when dealing with a multiple pregnancy. They then invite you to bring the babies back when they are ready for routine care and can see you for other problems anytime during the course of your pregnancy.

An obstetrician/gynecologist is a physician who specializes in the care of women only. These doctors complete the four years of medical school and advance into their ob-gyn specialty training, which requires four additional years (or more if they subspecialize in infertility, oncology, and the like). They have spent the majority of their postgraduate training focusing on gynecological surgery, obstetrics, and the general gynecological care of patients. I recommend that you seek a physician who is board certified in ob-gyn. Most of us with a multiple pregnancy will see an ob-gyn for our regular prenatal care and have him deliver our babies when the time comes.

When seeking your primary care obstetrician, arm yourself with the following questions:

- How long has this doctor been in practice?
- Is she board certified in her specialty?
- Has she delivered women expecting multiples?
- What sort of complications has she seen and learned to handle well?
- What will she do with you if she comes across something she doesn't know enough about?
- Who is her support network of specialists (discussed below), and when does she expect you to see them?
- What hospital does she use and how will they be able to handle your babies when they're born?
- How does she arrange for coverage after hours, and how does it work when you call her office with concerns?
- How easy will it be for you to see her or her colleague when you have an emergency?

While it might seem excessive to go to the doctor with such a list of questions, keep in mind that should you experience frustrations with your doctor's office, many of them will probably be due to a failure in communication. You may make assumptions based on your desire for medical care that is not in line with the reality of your doctor's practice style. If you know from the outset, for example, that when you call with concerns, you will speak to the triage nurse, who will confer with the doctor and call you back or provide advice within a framework of certain protocols, you will be less likely to be angry with the doctor for not leaving her other patients in the clinic to come to the phone. If you go into labor or develop a complication and expect the ob-gyn you see to be the one who meets you at the hospital, you will need to be certain that she takes her own calls after hours. By providing you with the answers to the above questions, your OB will be helping you feel comfortable with the quality of care you will receive.

Specialists for the Pregnant Woman

As a mom-to-be of multiples you will likely need to see a perinatologist, a physician who finished ob-gyn training and went into higher-level training in high-risk obstetrics. These doctors are also known as maternal-fetal medicine specialists, and their practice focuses on the prenatal care of women with high-risk pregnancies, such as older moms, women with diabetes or heart disease, and women with a past history of premature babies. These doctors assist your primary care OB in monitoring the growth and development of your babies inside you, and they have been trained to handle the complications of multiple pregnancy with which your OB may feel uncomfortable. The perinatologist should be available to you and your OB throughout your pregnancy and during labor and delivery, although she may not necessarily be present for the delivery if the OB can handle it.

Your primary care OB may send you to the perinatologist soon after your diagnosis of multiple pregnancy is made. Your visits to the perinatologist will likely be less frequent than those with your OB and may include ultrasound evaluation of the growth and development of your babies, a review of your chart and the treatments your OB has given you, and a physical exam to determine your risk of certain complications, to be discussed later. Once you know you are expecting multiples, ask your OB how often she expects you to be seen and what she expects the specialist to do for you.

Specialists for the Babies

Because you will be at higher risk of having preterm labor and delivering babies with low birth weight, you need to familiarize yourself with the NICU, or Neonatal Intensive Care Unit, at the hospital where you expect to deliver. The NICU is a specialized nursery for babies who are not able to stay in the delivery suite with their moms after birth due to any number of circumstances. In this unit your babies will be cared for by highly trained nurses, usually RNs, twenty-four hours a day, seven days a week. The nurses are supervised by specialty physicians called neonatologists who also direct your babies' care. The neonatologists often receive assistance in the NICU from nurse practitioners or physician assistants, but the neonatologist is the person with ultimate responsibility.

A neonatologist is a physician who entered a three-year pediatrics specialization after medical school, followed by extra training in the care of very young or frail newborns. These doctors sometimes have offices where they see patients, but most of their practice is in the hospital. Many parents-to-be do not meet the neonatologist until after the babies are born. While this is common, it is not an ideal situation. If your children require NICU and neonatology care, you will most likely find yourself too stress-filled to ask all the questions that could put you at greater ease when the time comes. Ask your primary OB for an introductory visit with one of the neonatologists who practice at your hospital. Ask for a tour of the NICU by the nurse manager of the facility. Introduction to this unfamiliar place will help soften the shock when you are faced with the prospect of your babies spending time there.

The NICU staff should be able to answer your questions about their presence at the babies' delivery, what you can expect after delivery, and what visiting hours and other rules exist for the safety of the patients in the NICU. Additionally, they should familiarize you with all the equipment and procedures performed should you be interested. If you took the tour and forgot or didn't want to know when you were there, refer to chapter 11 on NICU care. After your tour you should feel comfortable that the staff will take the time to answer your questions and will welcome you as an active participant in the care of your newborns should they require this special care.

When you speak with the neonatologist, ask her what her philosophy is regarding the care of your newborns. Is she interested in speaking with the parents? Ask her when she makes rounds, the industry term for visiting patients and deciding on the next course of treatment. Ask when would be the best time after that to catch her or if she plans to call each set of parents individually when her assessments and plans of care are made. You may ask to be present but you will likely be denied access to your infants during the neonatologist's rounds and the nurses' change of shift. In most NICUs the babies are all in the same room, and you won't be able to hear the discussions about your babies without hearing those about other parents' children. This violates the medical profession's strict rules about protecting confidentiality.

How Do I Find the Right Doctor?

This information may be all well and good, but what if you haven't the slightest clue where to start in your search for these doctors? The best way to find people to help us, whether they be building contractors or medical professionals, is to ask those who work most closely with the people we seek. To that end, call the hospital where you plan to deliver. Ask to speak to a labor nurse in labor and delivery. Tell her you are expecting a multiple birth and ask for a reference for an ob-gyn and a perinatologist. She is likely to give you two or three names that include the recommendations of her colleagues. The doctors most trusted by labor nurses are likely to be reliable, available, and approachable, and they are also likely to have a high degree of skill, or the nurses would not feel as comfortable in their recommendations.

As to the neonatologist, you are usually on your own unless you happen to live in an area with a hospital large enough to support more than one group of doctors in its NICU. You can ask the NICU nurses who their favorite neonatologist is, but expect them to be diplomatic. Most NICUs are staffed with one specialist on call for the day or the week, with the doctors moving in rotation, making it necessary for you to familiarize yourself with each one at some point. In this case, if you need further information, I suggest you follow the previous advice and speak with one of the doctors personally.

Ask your infertility specialist for references. If she does not perform her own perinatology care, whom would she like you to see? With which family physician or pediatrician has she worked most closely, and would she recommend him to care for the babies upon hospital discharge? Does she believe that your infants need to follow up with the neonatologist instead?

If you still need assistance in selecting your health care team, turn next to your sisterhood. Mothers of Multiples groups exist in many cities around the nation (see Resources at the end of this book), and a quick phone call or visit to one of their meetings can provide many answers as well as reassurances in this uncertain time. Moms are typically unflinching in their criticisms and profuse in their praise where it concerns the medical community. While this reflects more emotional content and less expert opinion than references from nurses, it remains a valuable source of confirmatory or contradictory evidence regarding the doctors at issue. Doctors who score highly with both nurses and moms will likely be a good pick. A doctor who rates lower with one group than another but who nevertheless possesses the appropriate credentials may require that inquisitory phone call or office visit so you may assess him or her for yourself.

Financials

One might think cost should be a secondary issue, to be dealt with at a later date, but I learned quickly how important it is to be prepared early. I was more than halfway through my pregnancy when I learned that twins were on the way. I was unable to continue working three months later, and delivered two weeks after that. My twins were fortunate to have been in the NICU for only ten days and two weeks, respectively, but I was out of work for over three months in all. It would have been nice to receive a supplemental paycheck during some of that time to defray the cost of three months off work, time off for doctor visits, and the cost of the equipment that the twins took home with them.

About three months after I brought my babies home, I received a bill from the hospital for more than $40,000 for the care of one baby while in the hospital. It took eight hours over two days and more phone calls than I care to remember to straighten out the mess and avoid the turnover to collections that had been threatened by the hospital. The insurance company had received a bill for two NICU admissions from one pregnancy and had decided the hospital had committed fraud through what is called "duplication of services." In other words, the insurer (who in the meantime had issued two new member cards with my children's names on them) failed to recognize that the delivery of twins required two separate instances of care and two separate hospital bills. And mine were boy-girl twins!

Supplemental Insurance: Although their numbers are dwindling, a few insurance companies still provide coverage that pays you for time off in the event of a serious illness for yourself or your children. In our area, AFLAC provided a supplemental insurance policy with a rider for ICU care. This policy paid for each day while the insured or his child was in ICU. In the case of the father of quadruplets my husband interviewed, the father was able to continue to support the family financially while staying home to help out, and the income from the supplemental insurance eventually paid off his house and bought his family a van to shuttle around his infants, solely because the babies had each been in the ICU for an extended time. See the Resources section for details.

Warning Your Health Insurer

Unfortunately, in our case, we had notified the insurer but the error still occurred. It was later found that the error was the way in which the claim had been filed by the hospital. I recommend that you, too, call the company, but instead of speaking with whoever answers the phone, ask for the claims manager for your region. Remember, the first person you speak to at any place of business is likely to be a person in an entry-level position who makes no decisions in the long run. He will not be the person who reviews the claim for accuracy or who will be able to help you should a problem arise.

When you speak to the claims manager (who is also not likely to be the first person who answers the phone in the claims department, so ask again to be certain), ask her name and write it down. Tell her you are expecting multiples and how many babies you are expecting. Ask her what you must do to assure that this is known when the claim is processed. She will likely type something on a computer within your hearing and tell you that all is well, that you need do nothing more. Now ask for her mailing address; it may be different from the one on your insurance card. Next, send a letter addressed to her, preferably by certified mail, return receipt, and keep a copy for your files. Remind her of your phone conversation and again notify her of your multiple pregnancy. While this might not guarantee that you won't have to go through what I did, at least you'll have documentation of your good-faith efforts should a problem arise.

Preparing Your Boss

If you are employed when you learn you are having multiples, now is the time to begin a serious assessment of whether you will remain in the workforce. If so, the question of where and how you will find child care will be addressed in chapter 13. The pressing issue at the moment is how you will tell your boss and coworkers, and how you can arrange for both a smooth exit and a reentry after your leave of absence. In my case, I was only in my first month of private practice when I found out I was pregnant. To say that my new partner was upset is an understatement. When I told him three months later that I was expecting twins, well, he was nearly beside himself. Despite my initial fears, I found him and my clinic to be more than willing to accommodate my condition. After all, what's family medicine about if it's not about the family? I remain in full-time practice at the same clinic with the same partner and have since had the opportunity to repay some of the kindness shown to me during my pregnancy.

Telling the boss you are pregnant is never an easy political move. Although notions of women's equality in the workforce and the presence of laws such as the Family and Medical Leave Act have made much about our lives easier, many of us are faced with the fear of job or promotion loss when announcing a medical condition that is inconvenient for and seemingly preventable in the eyes of the business world. To that end, many books and advice columns have postulated that it is better to avoid discussion of the pregnancy until somewhere in the second trimester, when your belly begins to swell and your condition is obvious to all. In your case you *look* pregnant almost as soon as you are because you're having multiples. You will likely not be able to delay the discussion as long as other women can.

As the bearer of a higher risk pregnancy, you may also require special accommodations sooner than other pregnant women. Your doctor may forbid lifting more than ten pounds, for example, but you work in the assembly plant. He may not permit you to stand for a prolonged time in the same place, but you are a lecturer and speak for hours on end. Whatever your job, ask your physician when you first meet what limitations he will place on your occupation. Ask him to put in writing what complications of your pregnancy could result from your continuing in the same line of work and when he thinks you might have to quit working altogether. You may want to refer to chapter 4 for hints on this subject. If you require special accommodations due to the recommendations of your physician, you may qualify for job protection under the Americans with Disabilities Act.

When it's time to speak with the boss, check with employee relations or human resources and ask them for copies of the written policies of the company regarding disability due to "illness," time off for doctor's visits and hospitalization, and whether your leave would be paid or unpaid for the illness. Especially helpful may be knowledge of the company's policy on sharing sick leave among coworkers should you have a prolonged time off work. There is no need to tell them any more about your condition than needs telling. They are there simply to provide you with copies of the laws and company policies that pertain to your questions. If you wait until you're showing, however, they will likely already know what you are asking—unless they just think you are getting fat. They'll probably guess regardless—people are nosy—but feel confident in your right to maintain your façade of "just wanting to know" for as long as you feel you can.

Once armed with the knowledge of your rights and responsibilities, it's time to make an appointment with your boss. Sit down with him and explain that you are pregnant and that you are expecting twins, triplets, and so on. Tell him what your doctor has required of you and provide him with your doctor's written instructions if possible. If this requires a shift in your work responsibilities, have in mind what else you could be doing. If bed rest or hospitalization rears its head, ask if work from home is a possibility. Ask how you could best continue to serve the company, and if you hope to continue in your job after delivery, let it be known and provide your boss with well-considered options for his present and future placement of you. Show that you are serious. If the last thing you want is to return to work but you don't want him to know, by all means, don't tell him what you truly think. If your pregnancy means the end to all your career troubles and you are finished working, good for you. Turn in your notice and rejoice while the rest of us labor away.

You may need to consider training a temporary replacement in anticipation of your early departure from the scene. While this step is fraught with not unrealistic fears of the loss of your "indispensability," it would be a good-faith effort to demonstrate to your boss that you remain a team player. At the same time, continue in your efforts to provide and promote new ideas for the benefit of the company's welfare. While none of this is a guarantee that all will go well or even that you will have a job when you return, it can't hurt to keep in touch with the needs of your boss and of your department's productivity.

Let your boss know that there may come a time soon when you will be required to leave work until the delivery due to preterm labor or other problems that may arise. Most people expect that one pregnancy is like any other and that your due date will be the time when they can plan on your absence. With a multiple pregnancy you will be different, and it would be a courtesy to notify your boss that your leading a project which is due six months from now might not be a good idea. Offer instead to help wrap up projects in your field of expertise that need extra attention to complete now.

But, by all means, don't despair! The majority of employers will recognize that you are a valued employee and will do what they can to accommodate you. Those who don't want to may do so anyway simply because it looks very bad to kick a pregnant employee to the curb just when she is most vulnerable. If you can, use this potential hardship on your career as an opportunity to spend time deciding what you really want to do. If you're doing it, congratulations! If not, enjoy the time you have to plan your new life. How many others have this unique opportunity?

Once you have in place your team of experts and have begun the navigation of the gale you've feared in your career life, it's time to settle in for the long process of actually being pregnant with multiples. From gas to gurgles, fatigue to fitful sleep, get ready. It's a long way from over yet.

PART 2

Keeping It Together and Staying Healthy

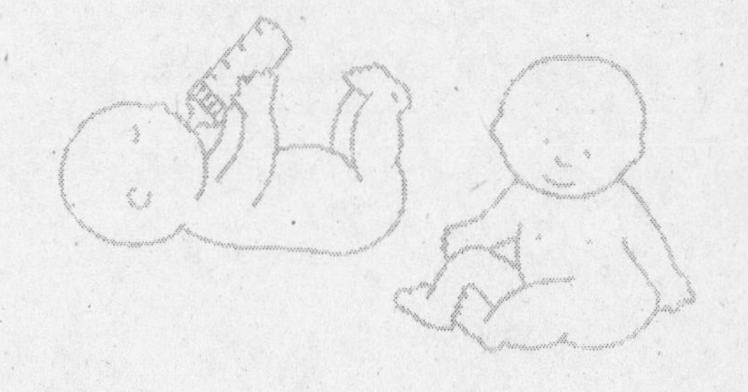

Three

The Woes of Pregnancy, or Too Much Milk of Magnesia Is Not a Good Thing

A couple of weeks before you were to have started your period, you had a date—either with your husband or with the fertility doctor—and whether or not you had hoped to be, you are now "with children." As many of us soon discover, the changes wrought upon our bodies in the next few months can do a great job of interfering with our general sense of well-being. The least I can do is help you understand them and make suggestions so that when this is all over, you can laugh about how miserable you were, because no matter how pitiful you are in your present condition, it is at least a finite reality.

Sometime at or about the time you expect to have your period, you start cramping in earnest; indeed, you may believe this time that you really do have appendicitis! You feel exhausted. Oh, let's be honest, you're physically devastated even with the slightest activity, and the idea of carrying a full workload is laughable to you. The mere mention, let alone the smell, of your favorite foods can cause you to reacquaint yourself with your most recent meal as it leaves your body. Your breasts feel like someone gave you Pamela Anderson's old implants against your will; overnight, they have become too tight against the chest and very tender. Sudden movement, such as turning your head, has suddenly become cause for the room to spin about you. You may not know what's up, but you do know that something is very wrong with this picture.

Those of us less than willing to admit we could be pregnant sometimes go to see our doctors, anxious to hear we have some dreaded illness rather than that we have become incubators for a human parasite. I have had more than one woman faint and/or tell me I must be wrong when the pregnancy test shows the little blue line.

Nevertheless, we leave the doctor's office having had the reality confirmed and holding in our hands informational guides in some form, whether books or bags filled with leaflets, introducing us to the world of pregnancy and to some of the problems we "may" encounter. Almost universally these guides use words such as "slight discomfort" or "minor irritation," presumably intended to help us minimize our symptoms and gain a sense of control over our body and the developments within. As you leave the doctor's office with guide in hand, yet another wave of "minor irritation" overcomes you, and you throw up right at the entrance to the elevator.

Anyone who minimizes the "joys" of pregnancy cannot possibly have spent time inside the body of a pregnant woman. You will likely be told the minute you let out the "P" word, by countless strangers (and just plain strange people), how much you should enjoy this experience, how special this time is for you, how wonderful it is to be pregnant, and how happy you must be. These folks either never had babies or have been afflicted by a hormonally induced dementia that has erased their memories of their experience. Nevertheless, they perpetuate myths that might lead you to believe this will be a cakewalk. I heard and believed many of them before my pregnancy, even while delivering other people's babies!

Top Ten Myths About Your Pregnant Body

10. You will feel little difference in your health or energy other than the occasional tickle of baby moving. In fact, you will feel better than ever!

9. You will be able to eat what you want, when you want, and will neither gain weight nor feel ill as a result of your actions.
8. You will have Rapunzel's hair, Anna Nicole Smith's breasts, and Hugh Hefner's sex drive, and will keep all three forever.
7. You will feel at one with Mother Earth.
6. You will prevent stretch marks by using the $200 cream you just bought at the department store.
5. You will be joyful at all times.
4. You will happily invite as many strangers to touch your Buddha belly as you wish to and be glad for the attention.
3. You will glow with the magical light borne by all pregnant women.
2. You will go into labor along your predetermined plan and take maternity leave as you had scheduled it six months ago.

And the number one asinine statement you may hear:

1. You will enjoy this so much that you will wonder why you can't always be pregnant!

Remember back in high school English class when you had to read about Hercules and all the trials he went through? He cleaned stables and fought monsters, and everyone thought he was so brave and strong. I would be willing to bet that if Hercules had to become pregnant and survive it, the boy would not have lasted long. Imagine Zeus telling him he had to puke in a bucket for three months, tie a discus to each nipple for nine months, be kicked in the belly every four minutes for five months (night or day), swallow acid six times a day for three months, and carry two cannonballs in his toga front while pulling an oxcart with the ox in it for twelve hours a day. No, I think Hercules would have cried like a baby to his mommy, who would probably have told him to suck it up.

Pregnancy, especially with multiples, isn't fun. It does not have to be the worst experience of your life, however. We have ways of making you feel better if need be, although we usually prefer you to try to tolerate

Keep in Mind: Doctors' recommendations for your symptoms will vary according to the region in which you live, and because all medications—even over-the-counter or herbal/homeopathic remedies—have the potential to affect the babies, I urge you to discuss any planned use of anything other than prenatal vitamins with your doctor before trying them.

your symptoms. What follows is a brief discussion of some of the more common ailments of pregnancy and a few of the strategies or medications that can be used to help you.

How Medications Become Recommended—or Not

Medications are categorized in classes A, B, C, D, and X to correspond to what we know or believe about their effects in pregnancy. We prefer drugs in classes A and B. We use those in class C cautiously if the benefits outweigh the potential risks, and avoid class D unless there is absolutely no alternative. We never prescribe class X during a pregnancy except in very unfortunate circumstances. We have few new drugs in the preferred categories because drug companies do not like to try out new drugs on pregnant women to see how their babies react—and few women are insane enough to let them try it! Keep in mind, too, that sometimes animal studies showing no harm are not sufficient to prove safety. Many years ago a drug called thalidomide was introduced into category B and used worldwide for the treatment of nausea in pregnancy. It worked like a charm, but then babies were born with deformed limbs. It is now category X and stands as an example of what can happen if we trust too much in the newer drugs at the expense of the known risks of older drugs.

Category A: Controlled studies in humans have shown no risk to babies in the first trimester and no evidence of harm in the second or third trimesters. Example: prenatal vitamins.

Category B: Animal studies have shown no evidence of harm, but human studies during the first trimester are unavailable or do not confirm this. No evidence of risk has been shown during the second and third trimesters. Examples: Amoxicillin, Augmentin, Zithromax (all are antibiotics); Tylenol; Protonix, Aciphex, Pepcid, milk of magnesia (drugs that ease indigestion, acid reflux, and constipation); Claritin, Zyrtec, Benadryl (allergy medicines); methyldopa (a common medicine for high blood pressure during pregnancy); Brethine (terbutaline) and Ritodrine (medicines used to stop preterm labor).

Category C: Animal studies show risk of harm to babies, but no controlled human studies are available, or no animal or human studies have been done. The risks of not using the medication must outweigh the possible risks of using it. For instance, a woman with uncontrolled asthma causes more harm to her babies by depriving them of good oxygen flow than by taking the medicines that treat her disease. Note that many of these medicines are used during pregnancy and that studies on some of them found few problems among the babies of women who had taken them while pregnant. Examples: albuterol, inhaled, or oral steroids (for asthma); most antidepressants; many blood pressure and diabetes medications; nasal steroids for allergies; Sudafed, Robitussin, and other cough medicines; many drugs used to control migraines; and narcotic pain medications such as Lortab, Percocet, and morphine.

Category D: Human studies have confirmed risk to the well-being and development of the babies. Benefit to the mother may outweigh risk to the babies in serious or life-threatening circumstances. Examples: most antiseizure medications (although uncontrolled seizures are life-threatening to mom and babies, and a few new drugs are category C); some antidepressants (particularly Elavil); some high blood pressure medications (especially those called ACE inhibitors or ARBs); and a few other drugs often used to treat serious illnesses (including aspirin, Bactrim, ibuprofen, and naproxen [Aleve]).

Category X: Serious harm will befall developing babies whose mothers take them into their bodies. The risks outweigh any possible benefit of the drug. These drugs should be avoided by any woman planning to get pregnant and should be used with extreme caution by any woman of childbearing age. Examples: cholesterol-lowering drugs known as statins; many chemotherapy drugs; Accutane (for acne); and thalidomide.

It is best to avoid all medications except prenatal vitamins or those prescribed specifically for your situation, especially during the first trimester of pregnancy.

Fatigue

You can now imagine what it must be like to be Superman surrounded by Kryptonite. The dishes are piling up in the sink, the clothes haven't been washed since the day of your last menstrual period, and your boss keeps asking if you are all right, because he has caught you snoozing twice during the lunch meeting and had to catch you once on the way out the door to keep you from falling down. You see the wake of destruction left in your path of inertia—and you couldn't care less. Or maybe you care, but you do not plan to do anything about it. You simply wake up, slog through the essentials of your day, and collapse on the sofa. Anyone who asks anything more of you must be itching for a fight because you are just plain *beat*.

Fatigue is one of the first symptoms of pregnancy. It happens as our bodies begin to adjust to the surge in the pregnancy hormone, progesterone, and to the shift in blood flow away from our bodies and toward the processes going on in our bellies. This is not only a physical burnout but a draining of mental faculties as well. Our thinking can be temporarily dulled and our concentration can be a little off, although I will be the first to tell you that I firmly believe we can still do our jobs well. We just tire out faster than we did when we weren't pregnant.

There is no quick cure for fatigue. It must run its course and will last for the first few weeks of pregnancy, after which it will disappear until near the end when you are tired simply because you have become unable to breathe. The best course of action is to listen to your body. When you are tired, rest. Go to bed earlier. The dishes will wait or your husband will learn how to do them. Understand that it is a necessary part of your pregnancy to do what will make your body feel better. Prenatal vitamins can help, especially those with iron supplements and especially if you are anemic. Keeping well hydrated and adequately fed is important, too, because your body is depending on the fuel you give it to generate the energy you need (see chapter 4).

Breast Pain

Welcome to the wonderful world of pregnancy. During the first few weeks of this adventure you will wake up morning after morning wondering who put the softball in each of your boobs. They will ache, they will throb, and they will grow out of proportion to your sense of what is normal. In fact, while you may like it later, depending on how endowed you were before this started, you may spend your initial hours post-breast enhancement trying to figure out how anyone expects you to sleep on your stomach, which is the only way you have ever been able to sleep before now. You may find as well that your husband has become way too interested in the events unfolding under your shirt. You will likely let him know that he will find himself quickly repelled the minute he places so much as a finger near one of them, since the slightest touch has become an unwanted addition to your discomfort.

You have discovered one of Mother Nature's last practical jokes on the female of the species. Although you grew what you thought were breasts during adolescence, until now you have possessed mere teenage boobies. Only the hormone shifts induced by pregnancy can complete the development of your breasts into those of a full-grown woman. After the first several weeks of your first pregnancy, your breasts will develop the type of tissue needed to make milk for your babies. As the tissue stretches and changes, you may feel bruised and battered or just plain *hurt*.

Like everything in pregnancy, this, too, shall pass, and you may even come to deny that it was that bad after all. Tylenol, cool or warm packs, and exercise bras can help alleviate some of the pain. Underwire bras (including my post-pregnancy favorite, the Miracle Bra) are frequently mentioned as causes of pain during pregnancy and should be avoided. They have been shown to block milk ducts sometimes, leading to infections of the breast (which *really* hurt—trust me).

When you are finished breast-feeding and your once-proud marys are pointing toward the ground, you may decide to start a grassroots movement for a national Breast Bill of Rights, guaranteeing medical coverage for breast lifts and implants for all women who have delivered babies. As far as I am concerned, this "deflated breast syndrome" should be considered a medical illness requiring surgical treatment. If you don't believe me now, you will later!

Varicose Veins

You may have noticed that your legs look like a map of the Mississippi Delta lately. Blue-red streaks have appeared where once you had skin. Sometimes they may actually become painful, and they certainly are not attractive. You begin to understand how Grandma and Mom ended up with such ugly gams, and yet you also understand why they refused to cover them because it is 90 degrees outside, and the last thing you need on your body is one more stitch of clothing. You begin to fantasize about one day having these veins stripped, burned, or otherwise eliminated, and in the meantime you highlight them with red marking pens as part of your grotesque Halloween costume.

Varicose veins form when the veins under the skin begin to peek out from underneath the fatty tissue that had been hiding them. They form during pregnancy for two reasons: one, because the volume of blood in our vessels expands, and the vessels must enlarge to hold the blood; and two, because as the babies get larger, their bodies put pressure on the veins from above, slowing the flow of blood from the legs into the body and further stretching the veins. The more weight we gain during pregnancy, the bigger the veins become, and the higher the likelihood we will have varicose veins. The more we stand in one place all day, the less chance there is that the pressure in the legs will be relieved.

The treatment for varicose veins is preventing them in the first place. Sit or lie down with your legs elevated as often as possible; this decreases the pressure in the legs. Avoid crossing your legs; this prevents compression on the veins in the crossed leg, allowing for good blood return to the heart. Wear control-top support hose if your doctor allows it. Avoid knee-highs because they can increase the risk of blood clots forming behind the knee. If your legs hurt, rub them with warm lotion or cover them with warm wet towels for a while. Take Tylenol if you must. Ultimately, though, how badly our legs look after pregnancy is inherited from our mothers, and some level of change is to be expected.

Stretch Marks

If you thought that your legs were beginning to look a little like a motocross racetrack, you haven't seen your belly in a mirror lately. When the babies take over the space between your rib cage and your pelvis, your midsection begins to attain roughly the proportions and the appearance of an overinflated basketball. The skin of the basketball has now started to thin, and you begin to catch a glimpse of the red lining underneath. Indeed, you may soon wonder whether the spreading red streaks traversing your abdomen are a warning sign that you will, as you have long feared, actually explode from the pressure within.

You may therefore find yourself on the Internet, at the health food store, or among a group of friends when the thought hits you that surely somewhere, somehow, someone must have thought of an ingenious way to make these stretch marks disappear. You may find yourself suckered into purchasing hundreds of dollars' worth of snake oils to rub on your Buddha belly in hopes of again attaining perfection (if you had ever known perfection to begin with). When you read the fashion and celebrity magazines, and sometimes the pregnancy magazines, and see these women exposing their post-pregnancy bellies, you notice no such badges of motherhood. You choose to believe that there must be a cure rather than realize that surgical repairs, makeup, and hours of photo retouching have gone into those images of perfection.

When we become pregnant, we sometimes expand beyond our skin's ability to stretch—and for those of us with multiples it is almost a foregone conclusion. As the skin stretches, small tears appear under the surface, exposing the redness of the connective tissue beneath the skin. After pregnancy ends and the skin shrinks back to normal (and, yes, it can if you are careful about your health—see chapter 13), the tears will shrink as well and the redness will fade to silver. Within two years after delivery, your skin will look the best it is going to look.

Although much money is made in the attempt to convince women that stretch marks can be treated, not even plastic surgery holds much hope for reversing their appearance. Like varicose veins, it is best to focus on preventing stretch marks. Avoid more weight gain than is recommended (see chapter 4), keep the skin well moisturized, and keep it well hydrated by consuming sufficient amounts of water each day. Although vitamin E oil has been shown to improve the appearance of scars, it has not been shown to be of benefit in preventing or treating stretch marks. Save your money on this until after the C-section when you will have something vitamin E oil can help.

Back Pain

September 2000

I was at the season opener for the Oklahoma University Sooners football game, in what turned out to be their undefeated championship season. I was twelve weeks pregnant and already bigger than I had expected to be. We had been invited to attend the game courtesy of friends with extra tickets, and my husband is an alumnus and a huge fan, so we went.

At Jenkins Avenue, near the southeast corner of the stadium, with thousands of other people crowded around us, we had begun to cross the street when a sudden fierce pain shot down the back of my right leg. Pain coursed through my lower back, and I collapsed in the middle of the street. As I was clearly pregnant to all those around me, I received a lot of attention. A police officer ran to help, and I had the feeling that everyone was looking at Ben and me as if to suggest he had something to do with my pain and fall. Ben lifted me, and I hobbled on one leg to the opposite street corner while the policeman held back the honking cars assembled on all sides.

I was mortified—but in more pain than I cared to admit. It finally eased near halftime.

I had aches and pains off and on for the rest of the pregnancy. Some days I could barely stand at my credenza to write patient notes; other days I found it hard to find a comfortable way to sit or lie down for more than a few minutes. After the bed rest and breast-feeding, my back was so weak and painful that I sought the help of a personal trainer and gym, where I finally found relief with exercise.

Pregnancy is often a pain in the butt—and neck and back and other places. As the babies grow, your center of gravity shifts until it is outside the body. You will have a tendency to lean forward without trying to and will need to lift your belly with your hands in order to maneuver in bed and in your daily activities. The back was built to withstand a certain amount of torque, but the stresses placed on it during the changes of pregnancy can be more than it can tolerate. I had often wondered how the backs of people with extreme obesity must feel; after developing a forty-six-inch waist in less than eight months, I believe I can say with assurance that I know.

In order to minimize how badly your back feels during pregnancy, you have two courses of action at present. The third choice, which is that you build a strong back *before* pregnancy, becomes a moot point if you hadn't done it before reading this book.

First, you must minimize the change you will experience in your center of gravity. To do this, focus on gaining only the recommended amount of weight, which will mean that most of the shift in gravity's pull will be due to babies and not to excess weight.

Second, you must maximize the back's ability to adapt to the changes it experiences. You must work on flexibility and strength. To increase flexibility, spend a few minutes each day in the following exercises:

- Sit in a comfortable chair with your knees at the same level as your hips and your knees slightly more than shoulder-width apart. Turn your torso at the hips until you are centered over one knee. Bend at the hips, keeping your back straight, until you feel a pull in your butt. Hold for thirty seconds and then repeat the stretch on the other side.
- Still sitting in the chair, lift your spine by imagining a thread pulling you up from the scalp toward the ceiling. Put your right hand on the inside of your right thigh and rotate your trunk to the left from the hips until you feel a stretch in your right side. Hold for thirty seconds and then repeat on the left side.
- Lift your right arm above your head and push it toward the ceiling. Hold for thirty seconds and repeat with the left arm.

To strengthen the back, you must work on your core muscles: the rectus muscles ("six-pack"), the transversus and oblique abdominal muscles (your waistline), and the paraspinous muscles (running up and down along the spine). Ask your doctor which of these exercises you can safely do (most recommend that you not lie on your back after the second trimester). Especially early in pregnancy you should be able to do all of the following. You will notice results in how you feel in as little as six weeks of doing them three times per week.

- Lie on your back with your knees comfortably bent. Slowly contract your abdominal muscles as if you were pushing your belly button into your spine, then lift your butt off the ground a few inches. Hold this for as long as possible, at least ten seconds, then slowly return to the starting position. Repeat this move ten times.

- Still lying on your back, place your hands at your sides. Slowly push your hands toward your feet, allowing your shoulders to lift off the ground. You should feel tension in your abdomen. Repeat the move ten times. Stop doing this exercise when you enter your late second trimester. Doctors prefer that you not lie on your back after that time because it may result in loss of blood flow to the babies.
- Get on all fours, with your knees in line with your hips. Look toward your feet, allowing your back to curve upward toward the ceiling. Hold this for ten seconds or as long as you can tolerate it. Relax and return the back to a straight-line position. Repeat this move ten times. Do not arch the back.
- In the same position, if you are able and have good balance, look up toward the ceiling as you extend your right leg behind you. Do not arch the back. Hold for ten seconds or as long as possible. Repeat with the left leg. Do this move ten times on each side.

Nausea, Heartburn, and Constipation

Among the first things you may have noticed since you missed your period, apart from the fact that you would just as soon sleep as anything else, is that you have become a human gas factory. From Miss Manners to Queen Elizabeth, every one of us has spent significant energy during our pregnancies in vain attempts to camouflage, to deny completely, or to otherwise devise socially acceptable methods for passing gas. Those of us who aren't the aforementioned important people invariably fail miserably and quickly poison our office mates in nearby cubicles.

When we aren't farting, we're belching. When we aren't belching or farting, we are trying desperately to poop. That is another of our curses: You may have been as regular as clockwork, able to schedule your day around your 9 a.m. bowel movement, but once you are pregnant, all bets are off. Your colon will seemingly have shut down, and no matter how hard you try—and if you try too hard, you know that hemorrhoids are soon to come—you can't seem to have a regular movement.

You may also soon find yourself ravenous and yet unable to tolerate the taste or perhaps even the smell of food. Your stomach is upset if you eat; it is worse if you don't. You eat Tums like candy, but you can't seem to get the churning under control. If you are truly unfortunate, you will be one of the chosen who spend most of their pregnancies hugging the toilet bowl.

All of these are symptoms related to that previously mentioned surge in the pregnancy hormone, progesterone. Among progesterone's actions, it slows the movement of muscles in the wall of the gut that are designed to help the gut move food from your mouth to your other end efficiently. Physiologically this makes sense: If it takes longer for food to leave your body, then your body can draw more nutrients out of your food, and you need more nutrients to support your developing babies. However, you are not used to this slower gut, so you experience the sensation that food is trying to come up the wrong end. You may actually vomit, and you can't have a bowel movement to save your life. This problem wanes in most women by the twelfth to sixteenth week of pregnancy, although the heartburn returns in earnest once the babies grow large enough to put pressure on the stomach to send its contents back up from whence they came.

In the early months of pregnancy it is best to try to treat this by eating small, frequent meals, sometimes as often as every two to three hours. Increasing fiber content will increase the chances of a good BM, and keeping food simple (not fatty and spicy) will decrease the chance that you will see the same meal again on the way out. Later in pregnancy, follow the same guidance, but add to it resting on your side on a firm surface and/or elevating the head of your bed until you feel as if you will slide off the foot of the bed. Your husband will just *love* you for it.

Among the medications recommended by doctors in my area are Pepcid, Tums, Milk of Magnesia, Protonix, and Colace. As with any medication, whether over-the-counter, herbal, homeopathic, or prescription,

I urge you to discuss your plans with your doctor before proceeding. This is where the subtitle of this chapter comes in: Never take more than the recommended dose of medication. I learned the hard way what happens when a person takes too much Milk of Magnesia. Let's just say I didn't leave the bathroom for three hours early one morning, about six hours after taking it for "gentle overnight relief."

Four

Nutrition and Exercise for More Than Two

How would you like to hear that you have the power to prevent many of the problems associated with multiple pregnancy—without having to be admitted to the hospital, without high-tech gadgets around and inside you, and without spending oodles of money you would rather be using to shop for baby clothes? Despite all your OB's skills and despite all the technological resources at his disposal, most are only designed to stop existing problems from becoming worse problems. We doctors are trained well in the treatment of troublesome situations that arise, but sometimes, no matter how hard we try, we have little to offer in the way of true prevention—that is, in keeping you from developing problems in the first place.

You, however, have the ability to improve your multiples' birth weights, their risk for prematurity, and their overall health at birth, as well as to improve your own health during pregnancy. There are never any guarantees, but your chances depend in part on how much weight you gain, what type of nutrition you receive, and how you handle your level of physical exertion.

I believe this is the single most important chapter in this book and have crammed it full of research information, for which you will find additional materials in the resources section. I strongly encourage you to talk over the recommendations you find here with your doctor because information such as this can frequently change and because I wish never to recommend a treatment plan to someone who is not my patient. You should find this chapter to be immensely helpful. It contains information that, had I known it, might have altered the way I handled my own pregnancy and perhaps would even have further improved my outcomes and those of my babies.

Nutritional Requirements for Pregnancy

The standard textbook answer for how much weight a woman should gain during a single pregnancy hovers between twenty-five and thirty-five pounds, more if she is underweight and less if she is overweight. Information about the ideal amount of weight gain for a multiple pregnancy was less clear until the early 1990s when a number of studies were done on the subject. What follows is a synopsis of those studies.

It is now believed that how much weight you gain directly impacts on how much the babies weigh when they are born. This sounds obvious, I know, but remember that we doctors have had all common sense bred out of us at some point due to our reliance on the "scientific method"—which has served mankind well otherwise, but sometimes we have had to do studies to tell us what our grandmothers would have told us had we listened. The goal for any multiple pregnancy is that each baby should be born weighing more than 2,500 grams (about 5½ pounds) regardless of how prematurely each was born. Such babies have a better survival rate and fewer long-term problems than do babies weighing less than 2,500 grams even if the smaller ones were further along in the course of pregnancy when they were born. (Okay, so score one for the scientific method in its apparent battle against common sense.)

As soon as you know you are expecting multiples, consider asking your ob-gyn to schedule an appointment for you with a registered dietician to assist you in preparing a diet plan that will provide the most benefit to you and your developing babies. We all know, intellectually at least, that it is not sufficient simply to add an extra bag of Cheetos or chocolate chip cookies to acquire the extra calories you will need each day of your pregnancy. Quality is of primary importance compared to quantity here, and the type of energy you offer your body to serve the needs of your babies is vitally important. While this chapter provides an outline of the basics, for many of us in our pregnancy-induced dementia, just remembering to feed the cats to keep them from eating each other has become a chore. Heaven forbid we should be able to figure out what to feed ourselves! A professional can assist you by assembling an easy-to-follow plan and providing follow-up care to be sure you are doing what needs to be done nutritionally.

To understand what a dietician can do to help you, consider the current risks of your pregnancy. More than 50 percent of twins are born preterm, before thirty-seven weeks. The risk that twins will be born weighing less than 2,500 grams is around 52 percent, and the risk that they will weigh less than 1,500 grams is about 10 percent. The risks for triplets and quads or more are exponentially higher. A landmark study evaluated the Higgins Nutrition Intervention Program, in which dietician supervision of multiple pregnancy was initiated at the time of the first prenatal visit and continued every two weeks until delivery. Adjustment in diet alone was shown to reduce the rate of preterm delivery by 30 percent, the risk of very low birth weight babies (weight less than 1500 grams, about 3⅓ pounds) by 50 percent, and the risk of low birth weight babies (weight less than 2,500 grams, about 5½ pounds) by 25 percent! Some of the findings of the dietician-administered program are included below, along with recommendations from other health care authorities.

In order for you to provide enough nutrition to support the growth of two or more 2,500-gram babies, you will need to gain a total of 40–45 pounds during a twin pregnancy and upwards of 50 pounds for a triplet pregnancy. We don't have enough data to provide reliable recommendations for those expecting more than three babies. You should ideally gain about 1 pound per week during the first twenty-four weeks, and 1½ pounds per week (or more) thereafter. In order to do this you will need to consume about 500 calories per child per day after the twentieth week of pregnancy above what you usually would require for yourself alone. For a woman of average height and weight, the daily energy needs are usually estimated to be around 2,000 calories. Moms expecting twins will need to consume around 3,000 calories. If you are carrying triplets, you will need to consume more than 3,500 calories per day just to keep up with the needs of your developing babies!

Women whose careers or living conditions require them to expend significant amounts of energy will need even more calories, but then those women will also need to pay particular attention to the advice that follows regarding adapting their activity levels to their new role as incubators of multiples. Again, while I don't recommend eating yourself out of house and home, this is not the time to obsess about how fat you will be after delivery. Most of us end up weighing the same as other women our age within two years of delivery. Those of us who are committed to do so can return to our prepregnancy weight or even smaller.

As pregnancy progresses, we require more of certain types of nutrients in addition to more calories to support our developing multiples. As with any dietary requirements, it is possible to get some of your needs met by taking supplements, and specific supplements are recommended for moms with twins or more (see below), but for the most part it is always best to obtain the vital nutrients needed through regular food intake.

The National Institutes of Health has modified the well-known food pyramid to provide dietary guidance for pregnant women, and although no firm data are available, it is believed to hold true for those having multiples:

1. From the dairy group: three or more servings daily of milk, yogurt, and cheeses. Be careful to avoid unpasteurized dairy products because of the risk of infection with listeriosis. Soft, rich cheeses are not allowed.
2. From the protein group: three or more servings of meat, chicken, fish, nuts, eggs, and beans. Be careful to limit intake of sea fish such as tuna because of the risk of heavy metals

accumulating in babies' tissues. Some say to avoid seafood altogether!

3. From the vegetable group: three or more servings daily
4. From the fruit group: two or more servings daily
5. From the breads group: six or more servings of bread, cereal, rice, or pasta
6. From the fats group: still to be used somewhat sparingly, but when used, select those rich in the essential fatty acids (see below)

A serving can be estimated to be the amount of food that fits in the palm of your hand, except for fats, which should be used in the smallest feasible amounts. Beyond these general recommendations, however, certain nutrients have been studied specifically for their benefits to help maintain the healthiest pregnancy possible:

Protein: Protein is vitally important during pregnancy. In addition to helping our babies develop properly, protein helps keep our systems functioning while the babies use us for their parasitic purposes. Although no strict guidelines exist to tell us how much protein we should ingest, the Higgins program with its positive results had women with twin pregnancies eat 50 grams daily, and another study showed good outcomes when mothers of triplets took in 100 grams daily.

Essential Fatty Acids: Fatty acids are the precursors to protein, which babies need in order to develop their nervous systems, organs, muscles, and other tissues. Without adequate intake of certain fatty acids, newborns can have impaired vision and nervous system immaturity, and may have trouble attaining enough muscle mass to reach their goal weight. The fatty acids of most concern are linolenic and alpha (α)-linoleic acids, which provide the most benefit to growing little ones. The best sources of these acids, some of which should be chosen each day as part of the diet, are egg yolks, meats, fatty fish, and sunflower, safflower, corn, canola, and soybean oil.

> The supplement Boost has been shown to help prevent Twin to Twin Transfusion Syndrome (see chapter 14).

Vitamins, Minerals, and Micronutrients: Several sources, including the educational bulletin distributed by ACOG (the American College of Obstetrics and Gynecology), recommend beginning iron and folic acid supplements from the moment a multiple pregnancy is diagnosed because those expecting multiples are at a higher risk earlier of developing anemia. After the twelfth week the Institute of Medicine recommends a specific regimen of supplements for all women with multifetal pregnancy. This supplement is designed to prevent deficiency in certain trace minerals and vitamins. It is recommended that such a supplement contain the following:

30 mg iron
15 mg zinc
2 mg copper
250 mg calcium
2 mg vitamin B_6
300 mcg folate (folic acid)
50 mg vitamin C
200 IU vitamin D

With adequate intake of energy from calories and attention to those particular elements of the diet believed to be of greatest benefit to your babies, you can help optimize the outcome of your pregnancy.

Don't forget that you will need to take care of yourself and your babies after pregnancy, too. Recommendations for nutrition during breastfeeding can be found in chapter 12.

Exercise

If you are among the well disciplined who are up and out every day for your dose of physical fitness, good for you. If you are among the rest of us, never fear: I'll yell at you about starting a healthy lifestyle to reduce your risk of heart disease, diabetes, and stroke—after you've delivered healthy babies.

Keep in mind that it is important to consider three types of exercise: aerobic fitness, strength training (muscle building), and flexibility training (stretching).

Aerobic Fitness: It is generally accepted practice to encourage patients who are physically fit to maintain a lesser level of activity during pregnancy and to encourage those who have been sedentary to at least begin mild levels of exercise such as walking daily. Exercise in a single gestation has been associated with easier and shorter labor, and although the interpretation of the studies differs, exercise does not appear to have any adverse effects on a single baby. The standard answer for how much one should limit exertion is that those with a singleton pregnancy should aim for exercise at about 75 percent of her previous level of training. It is known that highly fit elite athletes have been able to compete in their sports and deliver a healthy baby at term without complication.

What about those carrying two or three extra passengers along for the ride or run? Only one study was available at the time of this writing, a case report of an elite marathon runner expecting twins. Previously a 95-mile-per-week runner, she cut her mileage down to 65 per week and lowered her intensity to a maximum heart rate of 130 to 140 beats per minute (she would normally have exercised at 140 to 180 bpm). Three days prior to a scheduled C-section at thirty-six weeks gestation, she stopped running, and she delivered healthy twins. There you have it: One study of one lady who happens to run farther every day than I commute from home to preschool to work in my SUV. She still officially delivered her twins prematurely.

Since there are no other studies specific to multiples to guide us, we must follow what shreds of rational thought we have remaining. We know that multiple gestation puts us at risk for hypertension, preterm labor, and so on. We know that limiting babies' growth while inside us contributes to their risk of problems because bigger babies have fewer problems. Studies in single pregnancies have shown exercise to cause measurable, although reversible, reductions in blood flow to the baby, and although those studies did not show an adverse outcome, in our situation with our higher risk of growth restriction, loss of blood flow to the babies might not be a good idea.

Aerobic exercise has not been shown to induce uterine contractions in a normal singleton pregnancy, but ours are not normal singleton pregnancies and we've been contracting more than our sisters ever thought of since the beginning of this mess. The changes evident in a single baby's heart rate during exercise were shown to return to normal within two minutes after Mom stopped, but we have no evidence to say that elevated heart rates are safe for multiples.

I recommend a long heart-to-heart with your physician. If you are adamant about aerobic fitness and wish to continue exercise, I would recommend it only with the blessing of your OB and with careful monitoring by a certified trainer with a special interest in exercise during pregnancy. Aim for exercise at or below 75 percent of your previous normal intensity and stop immediately should you experience pain, shortness of breath, cramping, or any other sign of trouble. Unless your OB considers your high-risk pregnancy to be especially high risk, I believe a simple walk around the block once or twice a day, just enough to get your juices flowing and your body moving, is relatively safe and could provide you with that five-minute "heartburn-free zone" you've been desperately needing.

Strength Training: Strength training done in order to build muscle has not been studied in multiple pregnancy as far as I know. Although light weight lifting can increase flexibility, it can also elevate blood pressure and reduce blood flow to the babies during the time of the repetition. Unless your OB feels differently, I would save the heavy lifting for after the babies are born. Some light work on your back muscles or abdominals (in the first two trimesters only, or until your OB says to stop) can help reduce your risk of developing pain and disability from the shift in your center of gravity, which will move from your pelvis to somewhere in Kansas by the time you're ready to pop. Again, I recommend this only with your OB's blessing and only under strict supervision.

Flexibility Training: Maintaining flexibility is important during pregnancy, and multiple pregnancy is no different. Again, little knowledge exists in this area about safety for the babies, but your risks of injury during aerobic exercise or bed rest or labor can be decreased by simple stretches. I recommend finding a pregnancy-specific yoga class or other function that will help you stay limber. The breathing and relaxation techniques taught there couldn't hurt, either. Ask your OB for a list of providers in your area or for a handout on which exercises she believes are safe in your situation.

Bed Rest, or What to Do When You Can't Do Anything

By the twenty-eighth week of pregnancy—or perhaps earlier, for those of you less fortunate—your doctor may ask you to reduce your activity significantly or place you on strict bed rest, that is, that you be tied down to the nearest spot on which you land shortly upon your arrival home (or, worse yet, the hospital) and stay there, motionless, except to use the bathroom, until your litter arrives. She will do this not because she wants to torture you—although you may feel quite harassed indeed—but in the hopes that she can prevent complications from hypertension, preterm labor, or other condition that may cause you or the babies harm.

You will soon exhaust your feeling of blissful inertia and recall with frustration the list of things you had to do before the babies arrived. You will become addicted to television long enough to realize that it contains nothing during the daytime that will not reduce your brain to mush. You may find yourself, therefore, in search of things you can do to keep your mind stimulated while your body rots on the sofa. Ponder this: Do you really need to be on bed rest? Could you avoid having to go on strict bed rest by modifying your activity level now? Do you need to upgrade your cable or satellite service now or wait until your eyes glaze over from sheer boredom?

Thursday, February 22, 2001

Somewhere in my thirty-third week of pregnancy I went into labor. The pain was incredible—a terrible, searing pain throughout my whole abdomen I couldn't identify—and my uterus seemed to be constantly rock-hard. I couldn't find a "baby-free" spot to palpate to see if I was having contractions. As long as I didn't move or cough or talk too loudly—or breathe—I could control the pain. Considering that I had a raging upper respiratory infection, it can fairly be said I hurt all night. I had to beg Ben to hold my belly and push against it with a pillow just so I could blow my nose.

Ben took me to the hospital where I received three shots of terbutaline and discovered it to be the singularly most unpleasant medicine I had ever been given. With each shot I felt first the pain of the injection—which, by the way, hurts*—and then the prostrating exhaustion, fast heartbeat, and shortness of breath I imagine a heart failure patient must feel. I grinned and bore it because it was stopping the contractions that had indeed appeared on the monitor. I also learned that the ripping pain had not been the contractions but something euphemistically known as "uterine irritability." I'm convinced that men have made up most of these medical terms because I can't imagine a more underwhelming descriptive phrase for such pain.*

Now I lay here facing house arrest. The practice has been closed indefinitely, and I do worry about it, but I'm so grateful to have had the warning. I don't think I could have handled the guilt if something terrible had happened to the babies while I was still working. Apparently there had been a miscommunication, because Jeff thought I had already stopped working. He says he would have stopped me sooner.

Postscript 2003

Between the prostration induced by terbutaline and my feeble attempts at maintaining my balance on the sofa—with the two of them kicking me senseless (and don't get me wrong, I was grateful to even feel them at that point)—I finished the scrapbooks of our wedding and honeymoon and felt a sense of great accomplishment. Exhausting this avenue of productivity while in the horizontal position required all of a week. I next resolved to read every book I had—but only the ones not having any medical information. That left me with three unread issues of Vogue, *and I laughed to myself at the irony of a woman with a balloon for a belly comparing notes with the "heroin chic" set. I searched the Internet for information about bed rest and found many links to chat rooms, which I found myself intrigued enough to read but too intimidated to become involved with myself.*

My sanity began to slip from the sensory deprivation of many hours spent in silence, and I regressed to the pleasures of my college years in hopes of reliving some past fantasy life in which I didn't notice that I belched or farted four times per hour—which means, of course, that I caught up with the continuing drama of Bo, Hope, Marlena, and John, who continued in their fight for good against the evil Stefano. It seems that someone was sleeping with someone else, and perhaps some others were plotting the demise of another. I can't recall exactly, and it doesn't really matter anyway because I fell asleep halfway through every time. As I fell deeper into madness, I allowed myself the guilty pleasure of the morning "talk shows," if you can call them that, and understood what my husband meant by his defense that he watched the antics of Mr. Springer's guests "only to remind myself how lucky I am to have found you."

Despite my best efforts at complying with Jeff and John's advice, I went into labor for real in early March. Jack weighed only 4 pounds 7 ounces, Emma 5 pounds 1 ounce. As I listened for them to cry and later followed them into the ICU, I wondered what else could have been done to let them grow for just a little longer. Sending them off to their first week in preschool before writing this, I observed two happy, healthy, and whole children, and I gave thanks and realized that it had all worked out well enough.

Much controversy in the literature surrounds the subject of bed rest. Several studies have shown little or no benefit in the prevention of adverse outcomes, but, again, sometimes we do what we do not because we know it will work but because we know of no other alternative at the time. Studies have shown, however, that although we cannot prevent preterm labor by the use of bed rest, we can decrease the risk of developing hypertension and the risk to your multiples of low birth weight. There is, for the most part, consensus that hospitalization and routinely monitored bed rest are seldom needed except in certain special circumstances, such as the doctor's inability to trust Mom to cool her heels, Mom's inability to be near enough to the hospital because she lives too far away, or the need to treat Mom for other conditions related to the pregnancy.

What has been shown time and again is that certain of the behaviors we rely on to keep our jobs or our homes intact every day put us at risk of complications in multiple pregnancy. Several studies have suggested that it may be healthier for a twin pregnancy that you do not plant yourself firmly on the sofa but instead take it easy, reducing your daily activities earlier in pregnancy and staying at home as much as possible.

If you think the idea of reducing your activity level now (before you have had the spare bedroom cleared of debris and decided what color to paint the room) is asinine, consider this: Those of us (myself included) whose occupations required standing for prolonged periods of time (more than three hours daily) were found to be *most* at risk for preterm labor and other complications. Other activities found to be detrimental to multiple pregnancies are carrying loads of more than twenty pounds, working on industrial machines, doing repetitive-motion activities that were not stimulating, serving in military duty, and performing activities requiring exposure to loud noises, harmful chemicals, or excessive cold. Outside of improved nutrition, the most beneficial strategies for reducing your risk of preterm labor have been shown to be:

1. Reducing your hours of paid work with or without reduction in workload
2. Reducing or eliminating climbing stairs, carrying groceries, and doing the laundry
3. Avoiding house painting and nursery decoration
4. Instituting a two-hour rest period three times daily

Given that you are already at risk for preterm labor and so on, why not go ahead and use this as an excuse to get your family off their duffs to fix dinner for you for the next few months? Of course, they're not likely to believe you are trying to eliminate your risks if you spend your free time training for marathons.

Of those authorities that continue to recommend bed rest, or at least a reduction in activity, the timing of such a reduction has been shown to be important as well. Most of the conventional wisdom passed from attending physician (the big boss) to resident doctor (the little boss) to medical student (the "scut monkey") through the years has been that we should restrict your movements around your twenty-eighth week of pregnancy. This has not been shown to hold true in multiple gestations. If you believe your doctor will place you at rest at some point, ask her when she feels it would be most appropriate. Many of the problems associated with multiple pregnancy have been found to happen before twenty-eight weeks, and some articles even suggest limiting your activity as early as twenty-two or twenty-three weeks. It is recognized by these experts, however, that prolonged rest puts a strain on families, and for those without strong support networks, it may be preferable to balance the potential risks of continuing activities against the risks of financial or psychological hardship when formulating the best plan for an individual woman.

So what does one do when one can't do anything? Those who have nothing else to do quickly think of all the things they should be doing. If your doctor has told you to stop *doing,* then by all means listen to her and quit *doing*. Go ahead and indulge in your favorite quiet pastime that you swore you would do when you became that pampered woman of leisure we have all secretly desired to be. It may be the only time you have left to try it. Read books, write the thank-you notes from your shower three months ago, work on scrapbooks. Get on the Internet or see the Resources section of this book for chat rooms and information on multiple motherhood, or find the most expensive maternity clothes you can find, just for laughs. I found a company based in Paris that will fly over a designer to assess your closet, measure you, fly back to Paris, and deliver a maternity wardrobe to complement your existing one. The asking price? It started at $26,000 and went up from there. Considering that my pregnancy wardrobe eventually consisted of two badly stretched knit maternity dresses and my husband's shirts from before he lost weight, I figured I wasn't their best candidate. Besides, you can spend all the dough you want, you'll still want to burn the suckers after you're done with them.

Which reminds me: You might also consider getting the supplies you'll need for your upcoming event long before your doctor says "whoa." By the time you've been at bed rest for a few weeks, your brain will automatically begin to do the math about all that stuff you're going to need to keep the kids warm, dry, and fed.

Five

Preparing for Babies

It is my favorite commercial right now. You've seen it. It's the one for the credit card featuring the exhausted husband and wife of newborn twins who buy enough diapers with their credit card in all those runs they make to the store during lunch breaks, after work, and at 2 a.m. to earn themselves a date night complete with limousine, during which they go out and buy—you guessed it—more diapers. If you are expecting multiples, get ready. This is your life—sooner than you think.

Whoever thought they could afford to have children was either ridiculously blessed (God love 'em) or completely foolhardy (Saints preserve 'em). For most of us who learned we were having multiples, merely thinking about the costs of day care, diapers, and formula sent waves of nausea over us worse than our morning sickness had been. The thought of college tuition eighteen years from now had us positively petrified. Wedding costs for three girls at once could send us into preterm labor again if we thought about it. Never mind the long term—you have to survive the first two years with these darlings. Right now you may find you could use some idea about how your budget is going to change, and some tips on stocking up for the near future. The keys are planning . . . and presents.

How Many Diapers Do I Need?

Three hundred per baby per month, on average. That's right. You will be changing diapers every three or four hours, morning, noon, and night, for the first several months, and every five or six hours later on. That's six hundred diapers for twins, nine hundred for triplets, and one grocery store's entire supply for quads. Don't be surprised if you find yourself at the store every three or four days shelling out your hard-earned money on nonbiodegradable pants for your babies to poop in.

This may be your largest expense outside of the medical costs of caring for your babies; formula runs a close second. It pays to shop around. Some grocery chains offer points programs with free diapers or gift certificates. Discount diaper outlets abound with second-quality diapers. Diapers at such outlets are available for up to half the price of even the grocery store "no name" brands. I was even able to find more diaper sources on the Internet than can possibly be listed here. I recommend that you enter "diapers" at *www.google.com* if you are interested in having your diapers come to you.

"Never," you may say. "Only the best for my babies!" Indeed, it seems that the minute we become members of the "Parents of Babies Club," we are constantly under scrutiny from those looking to see if we care enough to put their little rumps in the very best. These critics, mind you, will be the same ones who try to tell you for the eighth time that you will have no life once the kids are born, crawling, walking, potty training, dating, driving, married, retired, and so forth. They are also the same ones who will try to convince your sixteen-year-old triplets that each one of them needs a Porsche as soon as their driver's licenses are minted.

Remember the tag line in the diaper commercial that wants you to "get over it, then get (their product)"? Right now is a really good time to get over it! Your babies will live in these diapers for only two or three hours at a time, and they won't be crawling around on the floor getting themselves dirty for a while yet. A discounter can save you more than half of what you would pay for the grocery store name brands, and until they have learned to actually produce enough urine to soak a diaper, you have nothing to worry about.

There is one more option, one that my cousin in San Diego considered for her baby who was born around the same time as my twins. You can put their behinds in cloth. She and I had an interesting conversation about which is more harmful to the environment: disposable diapers in landfills or detergent runoff and water use from washing the cloth ones. We never did reach consensus, but parents of multiples would have the advantage of reusing the diapers if they are able to find the washing machine amid the chaos. There is some suggestion that infants in cloth diapers are more easily potty-trained than those in disposables, but the evidence is weak enough to keep me from recommending them as strongly as I recommend breast-feeding, for example. Many big cities have diaper services, but the cost for multiples in my area turned out to be higher than buying disposables in bulk.

In the end, my husband and I felt lucky to have had the presence of mind to keep our twins' bottoms in the darned things half of the time.

Shopping for a Litter of Pups

If you're lucky enough to bring the babies home with you, you'll have no time to shop, and if they stay in the hospital, you'll have little energy for much except being with them there. Now would be as good a time as any to get your supplies for the crucial first few weeks while you establish your family routines. The list below should be considered a minimum for new moms. Remember, it pays to have friends with small children; hand-me-downs are good things.

These are the items your multiples should have waiting for them at home:

1. Car seats—the rear-facing kind, as expensive as you can afford. If you must skimp somewhere, don't do it on these items. Include them in your baby shower requests. The most expensive ones have sturdier frames, not to mention bigger cushions to soften the ride. They should include a five-point restraint with a strap that goes between the baby's legs and is

properly sized for preemies. The preemie sizes are often not found in discount stores, but there are some good Internet sites for them—my favorite is *www.OneStepAhead.com,* where you will find many items for newborns, particularly multiples. Do not accept a hand-me-down car seat unless you absolutely have to or you know for a fact that it was never involved in a car accident and is relatively new. If you have limited resources, call the children's hospital in your area to see if they have programs to help parents get car seats. The one in Oklahoma, Safe Kids' Coalition, actually gives away car seats to families who need them.

2. Car seat ratchets—the best new invention out there, as far as I'm concerned. Called Mighty Tite and invented by a dad who deserves every penny he makes, it is available at Babies-R-Us and at *www.babysrus.com.* This device locks a car seat into position securely with a minimum of effort by tightening the seat belt via a lever mechanism. In a country where three out of four car seats are installed incorrectly, it is not enough merely to have the kids in a car seat. During my training in the ER, I cared for twin toddlers once whose seats had been ejected from their mom's vehicle during her wreck. Let's just say that I cannot tell you strongly enough how important it is that the seat be installed *securely* and *correctly.* Any piece of equipment that can do this is worth your money.
3. Diapers and wipes—enough to last at least two weeks. That's 300 for twins, 450 for triplets, and half a grocery store's stock for quads.
4. Onesies—one-piece, snap-at-the-crotch outfits. Plan on each baby soiling at least three per day, maybe more. Buy enough for one week. You won't feel like doing laundry that often, and shower givers seem to love to give these anyway. A postscript: Save the cute outfits for church or photos, or use them if you didn't like either them or the gift giver in

the first place, because they'll just get ruined with daily wear.

5. Burp cloths—about ten per baby. These can be cheapos. Trust me. Even a shop rag will work as your little ones get older. Cloth diapers work well for this purpose and are inexpensive. The babies will use them for what they are, and in a few weeks you won't know whether it was a paper towel or your favorite blouse they just "urped" on.
6. Receiving blankets—three to five per baby.
7. Crib linens—two sets per crib, if possible. I learned quickly that when the twins' one sheet was dirty, it was just as easy to tightly wrap around the mattress one of those thin blankets everyone at the showers made for us. Just be sure that they can't get caught up in it.
8. Formula—if you are going to use it. I would rather you give them breast milk. You need to check with your pediatrician to see what type she thinks you'll need, because there are some formulas for preemies and for newborns with other problems that she might prefer you buy. I'd get enough for one to two weeks if it's not going to break the bank. One note: The FDA regulates baby formula as they do medication. The generic is as good as the name brand unless your pediatrician tells you otherwise, and there are no studies to my knowledge that show one brand of regular newborn formula to be superior to any other in the long-term development of your child.
9. Bottles—because even if you give the babies breast milk, you will probably find yourself pumping in order to meet the demand. Bottles allow dads and other family members to help while you focus on one baby at a time. You will need as many of these as you can possibly get, starting with the four-ounce size. Bottles are a great hand-me-down item. It is important to get new nipples, and to be sure to check that they are the right kind for your baby's needs. Check them frequently to ensure that they are supple and without cracks. Babies have

choked on pieces of nipple due to failure to replace the nipples regularly.

10. Breast-feeding supplies—a breast pump can be borrowed, bought, or rented. You will need storage bags to collect the milk and to insert it into the bottles for feeding. Follow your doctor's recommendations on this or consult the lactation specialist at your hospital. You will likely be provided one in the hospital while you are still a patient, and the consultant can assist you with getting one after you deliver. Also refer to the breast-feeding resources in the Resources section for help.
11. Antiseptic hand gel—to keep at the changing table to reduce the spread of infection between babies. I know what all the experts are saying now, that the use of these gels should be limited because they are so effective at killing bacteria that we may get another whole race of super bugs to deal with. I also know how difficult it is to change one baby, put him somewhere where he can't hurt himself, and then change another baby, all the while trying to be the good mommy who both supervises the kids at all times *and* makes sure her hands are clean between diaper changes.
12. Lysol and room deodorizer—because those poopy diapers will soon cease to be cute and will just plain *smell.*
13. Diaper Genie—speaking of smelly things. This, too, deserves a place in the Cool Invention Hall of Fame.
14. A really good diaper bag—ideally, one with straps like a backpack. Mine came from One Step Ahead and was about the same price as the department store brands. The great thing was that I could carry two car seats and the bag at the same time—and got pretty nice biceps in the process.
15. Bouncy seats—a lifesaver. They hold one baby securely in place and vibrate or play music while you deal with the other. An alternate in this category is a swing. We had only one, but it allowed one baby to be entertained and comforted while Mom or Dad provided care to the other one. Just don't use

them for more than twenty or thirty minutes at a time, or baby may get bored.

16. Other clothing items—depending on the season. Remember that preemie babies may need warmer clothing than their full-term counterparts because they have less body fat and a higher surface area. Consider long sleeves, layers, pants, and/or sweaters.

If you have gotten most or all of the things on this list, you can relax about the other fourteen thousand products that everyone else wants you to buy. You'll be busy enough without accumulating all the clutter.

Baby Showers at Bed Rest

So, you have this big shopping list and your last name doesn't happen to be Rockefeller or Gates. How in the world are you going to afford all this stuff?

The answer is: *Let other people buy them.* Unless you have lived in a hole in the ground for your entire life, you have at some point been asked to contribute to at least a few baby showers. You may even have been drafted to help host one of these festivals in which the primary event is passing around the pregnant lady's loot and providing the appropriate number of "oohs" and "aahs" while talking to your friends about how incredibly huge ("No, dear, you don't look *that* pregnant") the guest of honor has gotten and how her life is never going to be the same. You will have eaten dinner mints, nuts, white cake, and punch for the umpteenth time, and been exposed to the time-honored games of Whose Pregnancy Was the Toughest? Who Had the Longest/Worst Labor Experience? and When Are You and Your Husband Going to Have Children? You will have watched every grandmother there try to feel the baby move and will regret having had the urge to touch your cousin's belly at her shower because you are by now so tired of being public property yourself.

The good thing about baby showers is that you are given the opportunity to tell people precisely what you need and to ask that they get it for you. Even if they don't go looking for your registry, most people know what a new mom needs and that there are certain things she simply can't get enough of. Some of the best gifts at my showers were towels and receiving blankets made by hand by the shower guests. They were almost always softer than the store-bought ones, and several were personalized. To this day hooded towels with the kids' names on them—which swallowed them whole as infants—are employed in games of Superman and "hold me like a baby."

> If you are asked to have a couples shower, be careful. Most men still hate the idea of giggling over burp cloths and Diaper Genies, and unless the party is done very carefully, you won't have much fun because you'll fret about the fight you'll have over why he had to come in the first place. Know thy spouse and watch out for the pitfalls.

The point here is to let someone else arrange this party for you. If you are able to attend at someone else's house, all the better. If the party can be planned for early in your pregnancy, great. If you must wait until after delivery, fine. If you've been confined to bed rest, let the party come to you. As always, check with your doctor about how much excitement you can have, but in general, if you have to be lying down, comport yourself with all the self-satisfaction of a Roman noble reclining at dinner. Even if you have to be horizontal to enjoy it, you have earned it.

Once you have the babies' necessities in order, it's time to prepare for yourself. You may be in the hospital very soon, and you may have to stay longer than expected. The time to get ready for the hospital is before you are already there. This way you won't have to explain to your husband that when you said you needed underwear, you didn't mean your thong panties from college.

What to Pack for the Hospital and When

Singleton moms are encouraged to pack a necessities bag sometime in their last few weeks of pregnancy, to prepare the route to the hospital from wherever they might be when the time arrives, and to have contact numbers and alternate drivers arranged in case their primary driver isn't available. If you are expecting multiples, you might as well pack *now*. It is never fun to live in the hospital even if you are fortunate enough to go there only to give birth at full term, and you may very well be admitted one or more times before this is all over. The least you can do is bring a few of the comforts of home along with you.

Bring pillows. The hospital will provide you with a pillow slightly larger than an airline neck roll and made of some oddly smelling combination of plastic and foam rubber. If you are lucky, they will place it in a sack of cloth that feels as sandpapery and smells as antiseptic as the sheets on your inflatable mattress. At least ten other women will have slept on it in the past month, and it has to be constructed the way it is to decrease the transmission of infection from patient to patient. Trust a woman who has spent enough nights "on call" in a hospital bed because it was the only bed available to catch a nap: You don't want to suffer the indignities of a hospital gown sized for a twelve-year-old, and you don't want to try to get comfortable on a rollaway air mattress that never really lies flat only to forget the one portable thing that will remind you of home. If you remember only one thing before leaving for the hospital, be sure it is your favorite pillow. Even better would be your belly or body pillow, or whatever it is you're using to prop up that beach ball of a stomach that you never seem able to adequately position comfortably. Just be prepared to part with them after your hospital stay; you may not want them back in your home after you've delivered.

Bring food. It is no mystery that the hospital is no place to try to enjoy a nice meal. The doctors often order out if they have to be there, and the nurses bring their own lunches most of the time. Even if you have the good fortune to be in a hospital with a gourmet cafeteria, you will inevitably show up at the hospital at absolutely the wrong time to enjoy the fruits of the cook's labor. It never fails. While I don't recommend that you show up at the hospital and start scarfing while you're in labor—the very reason we ask you not to eat is in case something bad happens and we have to put you under and take the babies (because food on the stomach can cause vomiting and subsequent respiratory problems)—once you are settled in, you may be allowed to eat. From then until the cafeteria reopens in six hours, you will be offered crackers and juice because that is usually what is available. Wouldn't it be nice to pull out your favorite candy or peanut butter and crackers or whatever makes you happy as long as you have to be confined to bed? As a sensible person you will of course limit yourself to what will keep you healthy. Goodness knows I don't advocate blowing your gestational diabetes through the roof any more than I want to see a pregnant woman smoke.

Especially after you deliver and are cleared by your OB, have those foods you have longed to eat but couldn't have while you were pregnant. After the twins were born, we opened a bottle of champagne (yes, alcohol in the room!) and feasted on two wedges of soft French cheese, a baguette from the grocery store, and a bunch of grapes. We finished the meal with the darkest chocolate I could find. I ate until I thought I would purge, and I loved every minute of it! It was a true celebration, and as such the menu for me was so much better than mystery meat from the cafeteria. You will have earned this brief opportunity to relax in your newfound freedom to breathe and to digest without tasting your food six more times.

Bring personal items. The hospital will provide most of the essentials for your stay—if you enjoy Kleenex with the consistency of a coffee filter, sanitary pads the size of Nerf balls, and soap the size of a pencil eraser. The towels aren't much nicer, but if you think about what they will look like when you're done with them, you may want to dispense with the idea of bringing your best linens. Below is a list of suggested items you might like to see when you reach in the bag:

- Sanitary pads (maxis with wings, not just the little wimpy kind)
- Tucks pads (in case you deliver vaginally; trust me)
- Bottled water (you'll be thirsty, and you need the fluid to start making milk)

- Two or three dressing gowns (again, you may want to toss them later) and a robe
- Underwear (most of which you'll want to ditch later; they have to be big enough to hold those pads, so skip the thongs and satin)
- Shampoo, soap, conditioner, body lotion, and toothpaste
- Bedroom slippers of some sort (for traipsing to and from the nursery to see the little ones)
- Face moisturizer, makeup (if it makes you feel better, do it!), lip balm, and hairbrush
- Pen, paper, and camera
- Reading material (the daytime talk shows get old after a while, and TNT always seems to show the same movie five times in a row)
- Nursing bras and nursing pads (the thick round kind that are disposable)
- A contact list to inform those you love of the new arrivals (my husband, a computer guy, brought the laptop and e-mailed video and pictures from the room within hours of the new arrivals; I was still struggling to put together coherent sentences)

Leave at home. Jewelry will get lost, fancy clothes will be ruined (except for your going-away outfit, which should be a maternity outfit but can be pretty if you want), and your events calendar will be the last thing on your mind. Forget about catching up on your work or your scrapbooks now. You will be too busy pumping milk, visiting babies, sleeping, having blood drawn, and getting phone calls and visits every two minutes to have time to concentrate on anything requiring a modicum of concentration.

As you pack your bags, plan the baby registry, and stock the nursery, it is time to prepare your mind for the events that will unfold. You may have noticed that there are foreign beings growing in your abdomen, and they are causing more and more trouble the bigger they get. Wouldn't it be nice to be able to open a window on their world and see what precisely is going on in there? From conception to delivery, your body and your babies are undergoing some rapid changes. What is happening and what should you expect next? What will the doctor be doing, and what trouble signs should you look for? And, above all, when can you expect this experience to culminate in the ultimate endurance sport: labor and delivery?

Six

The First Trimester

It is likely you have just about made it through this stage, defined as the first twelve weeks since you got pregnant, by the time you purchased this book—unless you were fortunate enough to have known much earlier that you were expecting multiples. Perhaps you have experienced profound weakness and fatigue that laid you out by three o'clock every afternoon, and the sensation that your boobs were suddenly filled with lead weights that threatened to rip them right off your chest. You have probably lived off small amounts of crackers and juice, hoping against hope that you wouldn't puke again, and endured the endless cramps that made you think you were going to start your period. Meanwhile, as you settle into the idea that you are expecting these babies, you do indeed begin to feel pregnant and wonder what you can do to improve the chances they will survive to full or near term as healthy, well-developed children.

This chapter and the two that follow are designed to give you a brief summary of the changes going on within your swelling belly, what the doctors will be watching for, and what you can do to advocate for your little ones even before you can hold them. I would like to point out that every pregnancy is different and that, especially in a high-risk pregnancy such as twins or more, events may arise that will cause your doctor to alter what this book says you might expect. Also, there are few hard-and-fast rules for the proper management of a multiple pregnancy, so if your doctor tells you other information than what you find here, ask her about it and come to a consensus with her. By no means do I want you to follow the ideas discussed here if they diverge from what your OB says is best for your particular situation.

By the nature of the type of pregnancy you are carrying, what you can expect is that you will see your doctor—and maybe other doctors, too—more often than your friends who had only one. You will see your babies on ultrasound enough times to be able to paper the living room with their photos before they are born. You will also most likely be asked sooner rather than later to consider modifying your activities, up to and including leaving your job sooner than you had hoped. Thank heavens for the Family and Medical Leave Act!

Symptoms to Expect

During the first trimester, you can expect to feel worn out for most of the day almost every day. You may wake up feeling fairly rested, and if your breasts allow you to, you may feel a certain thankfulness that you can still lie on your belly—if, like me, that's about the only way you can sleep. However, the minute you ask your body to do something—say, get a bowl out of the cabinet for your cereal—you may find yourself ready to go right back to bed again. If your boss didn't already know you were pregnant, he may suspect it if he notices your running to the bathroom every ten minutes and falling asleep at your desk in between. As the fluid shifts around in your body to begin to support the growth of your developing babies, you may have a tendency to pass out if you stand too long or get up too rapidly. Be careful.

You will begin having contractions from day one and will have more contractions more often than those with a singleton pregnancy. I have heard it said that you are never so sure you are going to start your period as when you are pregnant, and whoever first said that is a genius. Everything about your body is changing, and especially if this is your first pregnancy, much of it will be sore for a few weeks.

You may also have more nausea than the average pregnant woman. The pregnancy hormones in your body are much stronger than those in women expecting only one. The pregnancy hormone progesterone slows the motion of the gut, and things can have a tendency to back up; if you are sensitive, you may find it difficult to keep anything down. Keeping a small amount of food in your stomach at all times (those small, frequent meals) can help, but see the section on what to watch for below and the Rapid Reference Guide to Pregnancy Complications in chapter 14.

What the Babies Are Doing

The first trimester is the time when all your babies' organ systems form. It is during this time that you must be very careful to avoid unnecessary medications, herbal supplements, and over-the-counter drugs. Much of the damage that causes birth defects happens before you even know you are pregnant. This is why we so strongly recommend prenatal vitamins to every woman of childbearing age and avoidance of cigarette smoke, alcohol, and infectious substances (including cat litter boxes) to every woman considering pregnancy; the absence of folic acid (available in the vitamins) is a cause of spina bifida and other nervous system abnormalities, and the presence of the other substances can cause poor growth, mental retardation, or other birth defects.

Two weeks before you miss your period, the fertilized egg divides and divides again. Each cell becomes a distinct type of cell, destined to form each part of what makes us intact human beings, from brain and nervous system to bones and skin, to heart, lungs, and other organs. The ball of dividing and developing cells then implants itself in the uterus.

It is during this stage of development that the type of twins or more is determined. If you are pregnant with multiple fertilized eggs, you will have dizygotic (two eggs), trizygotic (three eggs), and so on, multiples, distinct individuals as similar as any other siblings. If you have a monozygotic multiple (a single egg that splits), the type of multiplying depends on when the egg separates. (Twins are described here because higher order multiples from a single egg are so rare, although di- would become tri- or even quadri- in such a situation.)

- *Dichorionic (two placentas) and diamnionic (two sacs of fluid, one around each twin)* twins form very early—when the egg splits on the first or second day after the egg is fertilized. Each baby develops independently of the other in its own sac of fluid with its own placenta. Although these twins will be genetically identical, it will be difficult to tell before they are born.
- *Monochorionic and diamnionic (one placenta, two sacs)* twins form in the first week after the egg is fertilized. These twins do not form as completely separate individuals in the womb; since they share their placenta, they can pass blood back and forth between them and can sometimes have problems because of this (see Twin-Twin Transfusion Syndrome in chapter 14).
- *Monochorionic and monoamniotic* twins are uncommon and form after the first week. They share the same placenta and the same sac of fluid. It is these types of twins that can be conjoined (or Siamese) twins, and many have similar problems while inside your body that the above type have.

Triplets can be all from one egg and therefore all identical, can be from three separate eggs and therefore "fraternal," or can be a set of identical twins and an additional fertilized egg.

In the two weeks after you miss your period, you still may not know you are pregnant, but your developing babies have already determined the type of multiples they will become while inside you. Their nervous systems begin developing in earnest with the formation of early brains and spinal cords, and their hearts begin to beat. Ears, eyes, and early limbs start to develop, and each baby is the size of a small pea. Your ob-gyn will tell you now that you are about six weeks pregnant because we measure pregnancy as a forty-week time frame from the date you started your last period. Embryologists (scientists who study the development of life inside the womb) define pregnancy as the thirty-eight weeks from the time an egg was fertilized.

In weeks seven through twelve (since your last period), the babies form their eyes, ears, noses, and mouths, and fingers start to develop.

During this phase the physical changes that show whether the babies are male or female begin and will be completed by early in the second trimester. Chemical exposures during these weeks can alter the way the babies' genital organs look and function. By the end of the twelfth week each of your babies will be about a quarter of an inch long, and your friends will already be noticing that your belly is bigger than it should be.

When You'll See the Doctors

If you are an infertility patient or are otherwise known to be at high risk during pregnancy, you will have seen your doctor for confirmation of your pregnancy and will have a heads-up on others who don't yet know they are expecting multiples. You will have had ultrasounds to determine the type of multiples you are expecting and may have been sent to the dietician for the nutritional interventions previously discussed to prevent some of the complications of multiple pregnancy (see chapter 4).

If this is your first pregnancy, you may have taken a home pregnancy test and called your doctor for an appointment. Some ob-gyns have been known not to want to see you until you are past your twelfth week because one in five normal women will lose the pregnancy before then. In my opinion this is too long to wait to see the doctor for your first OB visit. The literature suggests that women at risk of multiple pregnancy (those over thirty years old or who have a family history of multiple pregnancy) should have an ultrasound as early as possible to determine whether or not they are having multiples, and that all pregnant women should have prenatal care as early as possible to assess the risk of birth defects or other problems for their pregnancies. You may go through this stage of pregnancy, as I did, blissfully unaware you are expecting multiples until the day of your routine ultrasound or until you or your doctor notice that your abdomen is getting a little too big or you hear two or more heartbeats.

Nevertheless, once the pregnancy is diagnosed, you will see one or more types of doctors. If your ob-gyn is a high-risk specialist, you will see only him; if you have a differently trained doctor, she may choose to continue to see you while also having you consult with a separate high-risk specialist. Plan for visits with the doctor and for regular ultrasounds, often on the same day. In the first trimester you may be treated like any other pregnant woman, with visits approximately once a month, unless you develop early health problems such as diabetes, hypertension, or hyperemesis gravidarum (see below and the Rapid Reference Guide in chapter 14).

What the Doctors Will Be Doing

Ultrasounds: These are intended to determine the number of fetuses you have and their relation to one another in terms of their placentas and sacs of fluid. It is too early yet to tell whether a baby has an abnormality or whether they are boys or girls.

Medical Assessments: Your doctor will draw enough blood to fill a milk carton and then, astonishingly, will want more from you later after you've recovered. She will be looking for your blood type and Rh factor (a blood protein that, if absent and left untreated, could cause illness in the babies) as well as other blood factors that may cause trouble. She will assess whether you have hepatitis or HIV, whether you have immunity against German measles (rubella), whether you have anemia yet (because chances are that you will later), and whether you have a bladder infection you are not aware of (which, left untreated, can cause preterm labor). She will check your blood pressure, determine whether you have sugar or protein in your urine, and may try to listen to the babies' heartbeats. Initially she will do a comprehensive exam from head to toe to assess your general state of health, including a check of your breasts and pelvic structures to see if you might have difficulty breast-feeding or delivering vaginally.

Every month for the first three months you will check in with her and have your blood pressure and urine tested, and she will watch for signs of trouble. After the first trimester she will routinely listen to the babies' heartbeats, using a handheld Doppler sound waves device, or ultrasound in the office.

What to Ask the Doctors

Ask now if you can be referred to a dietician. Tell your OB that you read in this book there are certain adjustments you can make to your diet that may prevent preterm labor and small babies. See chapter 4 for details so you'll be prepared to discuss it.

Ask whether you should have chorionic villus sampling (CVS)—especially if you are over thirty-five years old or have a family history of birth defects such as Down syndrome, Tay-Sachs disease, or other genetic diseases. CVS is done at about ten to twelve weeks of pregnancy. During the procedure, the doctor inserts a tube through the vagina and cervix and removes a small piece of tissue from outside the amniotic sac. The tissue is then tested for the presence of genetic disease.

CVS comes with about a one in a hundred chance of miscarriage and a one in three thousand chance of causing birth defects. For some people the risk of the procedure will outweigh the benefit of having knowledge about the pregnancy. For others the identification of disease or reassurance that none exists is of utmost importance. CVS is not a

Keep in Mind: Your doctor should always engage in what we call an "informed consent" discussion with you prior to performing any procedure she recommends, whether it be a screening test, an office procedure, or her preferred method for delivering your babies. This means that she provides you with the risks and benefits of the procedure, your alternatives to what she recommends, and the risks and benefits of those alternatives. You should have an opportunity to ask her questions about this information and understand well enough to make an informed decision about her recommendation before you agree to it.

required test for most pregnancies, even multiple pregnancy, but if you are interested, the time to discuss it is now.

Ask when you should expect to restrict your activity. Again, see chapter 4, but be prepared for an answer that varies widely. Ask specifically whether your OB expects you to be at bed rest, and if not, whether he predicts instead a lessening of your general activity level. You may find that this is the last trimester in which you will be without limitations on your behavior. Many high-risk specialists follow the recommendation that you stop working and reduce your activity as early as twenty to twenty-two weeks—and that's next trimester!

What to Watch for in This Trimester

Many of the concerns listed below pertain to all three trimesters, so I will only mention what is new in each trimester. If you experience one of these symptoms later in pregnancy, just come back to this chapter.

Bleeding: Bleeding can be a sign of miscarriage. If bleeding soaks more than one maxi pad per hour, call your doctor. She may be able to do little to protect this pregnancy, but she can help you stay healthy enough to try again. Bleeding during the first trimester can be a sign of vaginal infection. It can be a normal event following intercourse. It can also be due to implantation of the fertilized egg or to hormonal shifts while the source of pregnancy hormone transitions from the ovary to the developing placentas. If you should experience bleeding, lie down and rest, drink fluids, and monitor the situation. Call your doctor if you continue to have concern.

Abdominal Pain: Pain can be a sign of miscarriage. It can also be a warning of infection or of other illnesses, such as appendicitis or gallbladder problems, which can happen during pregnancy. If the pain continues for more than one hour or is severe, call your doctor.

Severe Headaches: Although we worry about preeclampsia (see chapter 14) later in pregnancy, high blood pressure can happen at any time and is more likely to occur in multiple pregnancy. If you have a history of migraines, these can be particularly difficult during pregnancy, but if you have a different type of headache or a particularly bad headache, call your doctor.

Bladder Complaints: Painful urination or blood in the urine can be due to infection of the urinary tract or vagina, either of which must be treated in order to prevent complications for the pregnancy. Frequent urination, which is a hallmark of pregnancy anyway, can also be due to the development of gestational diabetes. Your doctor will test your urine every time you see him because he knows it's hard to tell what is what.

Shortness of Breath: You will be worn out pretty much all the time, but true loss of breath from minimal activity can be a sign of heart or lung illnesses due to or worsened by pregnancy. Don't ignore this and assume everything is okay; tell your OB and let her check it out if you feel that your difficulty breathing is out of the ordinary.

Uncontrollable Vomiting: If you are unable to keep anything down and find you are losing weight or have a decrease in the amount of urine you make, you may be suffering from a condition known as *hyperemesis gravidarum*. (This means "lots of puking because of pregnancy"; don't you just wish we could speak English sometimes?) This is a potentially serious condition because your ability to preserve the pregnancy can suffer or birth defects can develop if you remain malnourished for too long. The cause is believed to be an exaggerated response to the pregnancy hormone progesterone; the same surge that causes most of us to be merely nauseated causes these poor souls to vomit uncontrollably. See chapter 14 for more details, but for now you should know that although women who suffer hyperemesis are miserable, their babies tend to do quite well. We're not sure why.

How to Prepare for Next Trimester

The "to do" list changes drastically the minute you discover you are expecting multiples. Reduce it to the most important items and delegate as much as possible. Begin the conversation with your boss about making your departure as smooth as possible while maintaining your job security as much as possible. Begin to plan and form your support network: Who can take your other children if you should be unable to provide for their needs? Who can help do the shopping, cleaning, cooking, and other duties? Who can provide help with travel to doctor visits if needed? Who can assist with the care and feeding during the first months of the multiples' lives?

If you haven't yet looked into supplemental insurance, do it now. Having the extra income while you or your spouse cannot work is of immense importance to your sanity. See if such coverage is available through your workplace or his.

And, above all, clear your social calendar for the next few months. You will be getting to know your doctors very well before this is over.

Seven

The Second Trimester

This trimester has frequently been called the best time of pregnancy, and it is often no different for those expecting multiples. We do have the added psychological burden of fearing the worst that could actually happen; we have heard the kinds of warnings from our OBs that our friends did not because theirs were not high-risk pregnancies. However, for the most part, you can expect to feel the best you are going to feel right now. The breast pain and fatigue have decreased, the contractions seem to have calmed down (although you will always fear feeling them again as preterm labor), and you look very pregnant without feeling too ill.

This is the best time to summon your sense of humor. When complete strangers try to make conversation with you at the store and you tell them you're "only" four or five months pregnant, they may look at you as if you are hiding the truth about the paternity of your child, comment that you shouldn't gain so much weight because you won't lose it again, or, worse, guess that you are carrying twins or triplets and diverge onto a completely new path of attack with predictions about the end of the world as you know it. Remember my earlier admonitions and simply smile—or respond with a great and witty rebuttal!

Symptoms to Expect

Expect your abdomen to swell like a balloon. You will look full term by the time you finish this trimester, and you will still have another few weeks to go. Expect your belly to itch as if you have poison ivy, and expect people to look at you funny when you pull your shirt up and scratch with the nearest sharp thing you can find. Stare right back at them and just keep scratching. You may begin to notice stretch marks as your tummy widens, and no amount of money can buy enough salve to keep them from coming. Most of it is genetics. Moisturizer can help the itching—if you can slather it on often enough and thickly enough.

You will begin to have trouble sleeping on your belly, although the heartburn shouldn't be bad enough yet to keep you from sleeping on your side in bed. You will feel the babies move earlier than those who have one baby inside them because there are more parts moving around in there. Initially it may feel subtle, as if a golf ball were rolling from side to side inside your bladder or as if your stomach is churning from indigestion. Later your twitching and tossing belly will become a sideshow no matter what the circumstances.

What the Babies Are Doing

During these thirteenth to twenty-fourth weeks of pregnancy, the babies are completing the development of their nervous and circulatory systems, and the bones and cartilage begin to form. The arms and legs mature into recognizable human forms, and the body grows in proportion with the head, which had been twice the size of the body. The babies will begin to make urine from their kidneys and blood from their bones like a mature human. By thirteen weeks the babies are moving their arms and legs, and by fourteen weeks they are moving their eyes.

Later in the second trimester, around twenty weeks, girl babies have functional uteruses and ovaries, and boy babies have testicles. Both have developed hair and eyebrows. By the end of the twenty-fourth week (the beginning of the third trimester), your babies each weigh approximately one and one-quarter pounds and are about 12 inches long.

Although at the end of the second trimester babies can survive outside the environment you have so graciously provided them, they can also experience a host of problems if they are born now, including mental retardation, severe lung problems, and multiple infections. If at all possible, your task and that of your ob-gyn will be to keep the babies inside you for as long as you can into the third trimester, when their lungs, guts, and brains will be more fully mature.

When You'll See the Doctors

In a singleton pregnancy you could expect to see your obstetrician every month for the first thirty-two weeks, every two weeks until thirty-six weeks, and weekly thereafter until you deliver. During the second trimester of multiple pregnancy, one of the only deviances from this pattern is that you will begin having serial ultrasound examination along with your office visits. You will see the doctor more often if you develop complications that he has to monitor (see chapter 14).

What the Doctors Will Be Doing

Ultrasounds: During the second trimester the OB will use ultrasound to better assess the type of multiple gestation you are carrying. Careful measurements of your babies will be done to estimate their size in comparison to one another and to normal values for their age group. The position and characteristics of the placenta and amniotic sac will be determined for each child in order to predict risks for each one during the pregnancy. In addition, each baby will be examined closely to look for signs of birth defects.

The ultrasounds will be repeated about every three or four weeks unless the doctor suspects trouble, in which case she may suggest that you have them every two weeks. This would especially be the case if the doctor believes that one baby is receiving more nutrition than the other (a situation called twin-twin transfusion syndrome; see chapter 14) or if she believes neither is getting enough nutrition (called intrauterine growth retardation; see next chapter).

Medical Assessments: Even with everything mentioned here, the second trimester is relatively quiet from the standpoint of medical intervention. You will be asked if you would like to participate in screening tests for Down syndrome or for spina bifida and other nerve abnormalities. This is done through blood tests and/or by the use of amniocentesis, a process in which fluid is removed from around the babies within the uterus and tested for the presence of abnormal genetic material. You may have more blood drawn to watch for the development of anemia or gestational diabetes.

The screening tests mentioned come with a few risks that you should understand before having them (always remember the information in the last chapter on your right to informed consent). Like all screening tests, the initial blood test, called a "maternal triple screen" or a "maternal serum alpha-fetoprotein" (MSAFP), is designed to be the least invasive way to detect babies who have abnormalities. As a result there will be more false-positive tests (meaning the test suggests a problem when none exists) than there are false-negative tests (meaning the test tells you everything is fine when it isn't). If you have a negative result to the screening test, we usually do not recommend that further testing be done. If the test is positive, suggesting that you are at risk of carrying one or more babies with Down syndrome, spina bifida, or other abnormalities, you will be asked to have more evaluation done. This evaluation consists of a high-resolution ultrasound to look for features of the heart, brain, face, and other areas of each baby that suggest Down syndrome or nervous system diseases, with or without an amniocentesis.

The risk when having an amniocentesis is small, but the possibility exists that the needle could strike one or more babies, causing injury or deformity, or infection in the uterus, as a result of the needle passing bacteria through the skin. There is an even smaller risk (less than one in a hundred in the second trimester) of miscarriage due to the procedure. I tell my patients when having an informed consent discussion about the screening for Down syndrome and nervous system abnormalities that it comes down to what they wish to do with the information. If they wish to have advance warning of the potential for having a child with special needs so they can plan ahead for those needs or if they might terminate the pregnancy, they probably want the test. If they would not terminate a pregnancy but would worry themselves sick about the knowledge they have about their baby, they might consider skipping the test. This advice does not apply to my pregnant patients who are thirty-five years or older when they deliver. I recommend at least the blood test to all those women because they have a much higher risk of having a baby with Down syndrome than their younger counterparts.

For those special populations of people at risk for genetic diseases, your doctor will likely recommend blood work to determine whether you carry sickle cell or Tay-Sachs disease, especially if you are at risk but didn't choose the chorionic villus sampling procedure. Other genetic tests are available for your specific situation (Huntington's disease, etc.) but are beyond the scope of this book. Ask your doctor if you have concerns about a specific disease that runs in your family or your ethnic group.

As with the possibility that you would have more frequent ultrasounds if the OB is concerned about your babies' health, you may expect more frequent office visits should you develop high blood pressure, diabetes, or other problems.

Your doctor may now reassess the level of physical activity in which you engage in your daily life. Remember that you were warned last trimester! Some experts recommend a lessening of physical activity beginning in the twenty-second week; others recommend complete bed rest, and still others eschew the idea of bed rest altogether, citing a lack of evidence for its effectiveness in preventing preterm labor or delivery. Speak openly with your doctor about your concerns on this subject and see where his practice philosophy lies. If he tells you to slow down, by all means do it. It is preferable to sacrifice a little now than have the "what-ifs" for the rest of your life should you not comply with his request.

What to Ask the Doctors

Ask that they explain to you what type of multiples you are carrying and what kinds of problems you might expect as a result. Ask what you can do, if anything, to reduce the risk of complications: stress reduction, dietary changes, activity modification, or other intervention. Ask about any symptoms you are having—even if you fear they may seem trivial to the doctor.

Now is the time to ask if your doctor recommends that you visit the hospital or NICU for a tour and whether she thinks it would be helpful for you to interview one of the neonatologists on staff for predelivery counseling. See chapter 2 for tips on what questions to ask.

What to Watch for in This Trimester

Bleeding: In the second trimester bleeding can still mean miscarriage or preterm labor. It may also mean you have a condition in which a placenta is separating from the uterus, known as placental abruption, or in which it is overlying the opening to the cervix, known as placenta previa. Either condition can be life threatening for your babies. An additional cause of bleeding is preterm labor or cervical incompetence, in which the cervix opens and lets the babies deliver too early, even in the absence of contractions. If you have bleeding during the second trimester, by all means tell your physician as soon as possible. It may be that your bleeding was from another source, such as an irritated cervix from intercourse, but these other conditions need to be eliminated as suspects first.

Abdominal Pain: In addition to the causes of pain listed in the first trimester, pain in the second trimester can be a sign of preterm labor, placental abruption, or uterine infection. It can also be due to something euphemistically called "uterine irritability" in which the uterus contracts in a completely uncoordinated fashion. Irritability may be a sign of infection, preterm labor, or other conditions that should be treated, but believe me, if you experience this, you will not fail to call your doctor.

Swelling: Especially in the face and hands, this can be a sign of preeclampsia, kidney disease, or heart trouble associated with pregnancy. If your hands swell, especially if they swell suddenly and you are unable to wear your jewelry, notify your OB.

Decreased Fetal Movement: It may be difficult to tell which baby is moving and which is not, but keep track as best as you can. If you feel less movement than you are used to, first find a quiet room, away from television and other distractions, and lie on your side. Drink something sweet such as juice or milk and pay close attention to movements for the next hour. If you do not feel ten movements within an hour, call your doctor for more advice.

How to Prepare for the Next Trimester

You are now in the homestretch. Chances are you have less than two months left on a twin pregnancy and less than six weeks left on a triplet pregnancy. Plan to go home sometime during this trimester and stay there. Activate the support network as soon as you need it and remember them all next Christmas.

Be certain you are receiving the best nutrition you can. Read chapter 4 and follow the advice found there about your calorie intake, your recommended weight gain, and the supplements you should take. Follow your doctor's advice regarding limitations on your activities, and get ready. The fun (if you wish to call it that) is just starting.

Eight

The Third Trimester

Here you sit, most likely on house arrest now on the advice of your doctor who hopes to keep you from delivering too early. This is the third trimester, defined as weeks twenty-four to forty from your last period, and although you will be thrilled to have made it this far, you will be counting the days until the ordeal is over. Each day during these three months comes as a blessing to you because you know that every day your babies are able to remain inside you and make you miserable is one less day they will have to stay in the NICU. You are officially on the homestretch.

Symptoms to Expect

You can expect to feel pretty useless during the third trimester. You will spend more time lying on the sofa with pillows above, below, and around your bloated carcass than you will spend doing anything else. Only rarely will a mom of multiples still be up and running by the end of pregnancy.

You will have discovered by now that surviving this long with healthy babies has come at a price: You can't lie flat without tasting your dinner from two days before, you can't move about without lifting your belly with your hands first, and you haven't taken a deep breath in as long as you can remember. You and your multiples have become a human anchor, sinking in the bathtub, onto the sofa, into the car seat, and anywhere else you may land. Weighing anchor to move from place to place will have become a feat of engineering not seen since they built the Golden Gate Bridge.

You will probably have begun cramping again in earnest by sometime in the early part of this trimester, which is one reason your doctor has sent you home to wait out the rest of the pregnancy. Sleep will come in fits and spurts as you seek to get comfortable, and you may begin to believe that this is some sick person's idea of preparing you for the sleepless nights you'll have once the kids arrive.

At some point you will go into labor, unless you and your doctors have decided to take the babies by C-section, which has become a distinct possibility you have had to consider.

What the Babies Are Doing

Until the thirty-second week or so, your babies have followed the same expected curves of growth and development as singletons. After that they begin to run out of room, and their growth rate decelerates. This is known as intrauterine growth retardation (IUGR), and it can lead to their being a little more fragile at birth than singletons of the same gestational age. However, babies with IUGR have been shown to have better lung maturity at earlier gestational ages due to the added stress they experience, and your multiples have a better chance of being able to breathe at younger ages than singletons because of this.

By the twenty-fourth week babies begin to make surfactant, an important protein in the lungs necessary for the lungs to take oxygen from the air into the bloodstream. They also have fingernails by twenty-four weeks, and by twenty-six to twenty-nine weeks babies have good chances of survival outside the womb if given intensive care. At twenty-six weeks babies' eyes open, and their hair and toenails have grown. By twenty-nine weeks they have started to store fat under their skin, and the fine blood vessels disappear under this layer of protection.

By thirty weeks the babies' pupils reflect light. By thirty-five weeks they can grasp items with their hands and turn toward light sources. Sometime between thirty-four and thirty-six weeks babies become able to coordinate their eating with their breathing, called the "suck-swallow-breathe" reflex. Babies born before this reflex matures but after they reach lung maturity will go to the nursery until they learn how to eat, and such babies are often referred to as "feeder-growers" (see chapter 15).

After thirty-six weeks babies have pretty much attained all they need in order to survive in the outside world. The average singleton baby is born weighing around 7½ pounds; the average twin, due to IUGR, weighs around 6 pounds if born at thirty-eight weeks. Triplets rarely make it to thirty-eight weeks and weigh even less at birth.

When You'll See the Doctors

After the twenty-fourth week you will see your doctor about every other week until thirty-two weeks or so, after which you will likely see him every week. Some doctors add weekly nonstress tests and/or biophysical profiles (see below) as a routine precaution, while others advocate their use only if they have concern for your health or the health of the babies that might cause them to decide to deliver them earlier than expected.

What the Doctors Will Be Doing

Ultrasounds: You will be on a first-name basis with every ultrasound tech at the hospital or clinic by the time this is over, and you will have seen your babies enough times to have an idea of what they look like before you meet them face-to-face. The doctors will continue to measure the growth of each baby in relation to itself and in comparison to its siblings to watch for IUGR or whether one baby is receiving nutrition or fluid at the expense of another. A special type of ultrasound test that may be performed is a biophysical profile (BPP). A BPP consists of a measurement of the fluid around each baby, the breathing patterns and heart rate of each one as well as muscle tone and movement patterns of each. This is combined with the nonstress test (see below) for a perfect score of ten out of ten. Eight to ten points are considered normal and a sign of health for the pregnancy.

Nonstress Test: This may be performed weekly or biweekly if your doctor believes it is helpful in monitoring your pregnancy. During this test you lie on a bed with belts around your abdomen that measure each baby's heart rate and your contraction pattern, if any. You may be given a button to push when you feel movement. A normal test consists of each baby's having two movements lasting fifteen seconds each in which his heart rate rises by fifteen beats per minute above his usual heart rate. This test can be done alone or in combination with the BPP (in which it accounts for two of the ten points).

Medical Assessments: Around the twenty-fourth to twenty-eighth week of your pregnancy, unless your doctor has had reason for concern earlier, she will have you drink something akin to flat orange Gatorade and will draw blood as a screening test for gestational diabetes. She will recheck your blood count for anemia and monitor you for the development of high blood pressure, preeclampsia, and other problems (see chapter 14 for common problems you may encounter during pregnancy).

Before you are expected to deliver, she will place a swab in your vagina and rectum to test for Group B streptococcus (GBS). GBS is a bacterium that lives in many of us and never causes trouble for us. It is, however, one of the leading causes of infection-related death and disability in newborns and can be prevented if found before labor begins. If you are positive for the infection, you will be given antibiotics during labor. If not, you have no worries about this.

What to Ask the Doctors

Ask when he expects you to deliver. Ask whether you should deliver vaginally or by C-section. In most cases we advocate vaginal delivery only for pregnancies in which both babies are head-down, or "vertex lie," although in certain circumstances babies in other arrangements can be born vaginally depending on your past obstetric history and the comfort level of your ob-gyn.

Be certain you understand the symptoms your ob-gyn wants you to watch out for. Read on, and ask him if there is anything else he wants to know about should they occur.

What to Watch for in This Trimester

Bleeding: In most cases a small amount of bleeding will accompany labor. This is called "bloody show" and usually consists of a mucous discharge with blood in it. Bleeding that soaks a pad in an hour or happens in the presence of pain that is unrelenting or is different from what you believe labor pain should be is a signal for you to call your doctor. The separation of the placenta from the uterus (abruption) and bleeding of a placenta that lies over the cervix (previa) can still happen and are still potentially life threatening for you and the babies.

Abdominal Pain: Contractions are typically a "come-and-go" affair, getting stronger and more painful as labor progresses. Severe pain that does not let up or pain in the presence of fever should prompt you to call the doctor. Pain due to contractions is managed depending on how far along you are in the pregnancy. Before thirty-six weeks we generally want to know if you have pain every ten minutes for an hour. At term we want to know when you have pain that is five minutes apart and regular for an hour, unless your OB is planning a C-section, in which case he may want to know sooner to avoid the chances of an unwanted vaginal delivery.

Swelling: You will have tree trunks for legs before this is done, but sudden swelling of the face or hands should lead you to call the OB. Preeclampsia (see chapter 14) is defined as hypertension plus edema (swelling), so if you have been battling high blood pressure this whole time and you suddenly swell, call the doctor immediately.

Decreased Fetal Movement: As it was in the second trimester, it may be quite difficult indeed to sense when the babies are and are not moving. There is less and less room, but if you are concerned, follow the advice in the previous chapter and call your doctor.

Leaking from the Vagina: Even if you think it may be just urine dripping down your leg, if you leak fluid, call your doctor. Your water may have just broken.

How to Prepare for What Comes Next

The only thing left to prepare for is parenthood. Your next focus will be on the process known as labor and delivery, otherwise known as the period after which you can breathe again, just before the period in which you lose sleep again.

Nine

Labor and Delivery

Those of us who have been pregnant know the sinking feeling, sometime near the end, that we have been duped. Somehow we were fooled into joining the herd of other lemmings racing to hurl ourselves off the cliff onto the jagged rocks below. Maybe it was the smell of baby powder, the appeal of the ubiquitous diaper ads, or the guilt complex given us by our mothers who reminded us incessantly that they deserve grandchildren. In any case, here we are now, facing what we all fear will be the messiest and most painful experience of our lives. As we try to prepare mentally for labor—and just so you know, you can't "mentally prepare" for labor except to decide that it is gonna hurt and you're gonna get through it—many of us question our very sanity at the time we made the decision to have sex (even if we had to have that sex with a test tube in order to get pregnant in the first place).

Overall, the end of pregnancy is never the most pleasant of prospects, but if you have survived the mind-numbing boredom of months of bed rest, the "discomfort" (what a great euphemism!) of terbutaline (a medication I explain on page 169), or the dismay of watching what could have been a cute pregnant belly swell to the size of a midsize sedan, you know you're expecting the multiplied fun known only to those in the animal world who regularly bear a litter of pups. Kiss the dog now; she has earned your respect.

The paradox is that those of us who have completed the journey of childbirth have almost universally expressed the ridiculous desire to do it again later—or at least the belief that maybe it wasn't all that bad in the end. I suppose that something about our evolutionary heritage requires the adult female to adopt some sort of episodic hormonal insanity in order to preserve the species. While you, too, can expect to suffer both the cliff dive of childbirth (although we have lots of cool toys now to decrease the pain, discussed in this chapter) and the later dementia that might drive you to "try for more," right now you need to understand how to best prepare for and protect this pregnancy for as long as possible to give your babies the best chance at survival and long-term health. With good care and a little luck, odds are that you'll be blessed with success in this transition and need only fear your possible residence in the nuthouse when the multiples decide to split up in the middle of the mall and see which one you chase.

Detection of Term and Preterm Labor Signs

You are in the homestretch—or you are far from it yet and need to know what to do. You feel more than the usual miseries of your pregnancy, and you worry. You feel more or less movement than is usual for you, and you worry. The insistent pounding on your cervix and bladder from two or more ridiculous children who want your attention has ceased to be cute (was it ever?), and you wonder: When is this more than a passing problem? Are you in labor? Should you panic?

The first step after careful attention to your own health during a multiple pregnancy is to recognize early when things might not be going as smoothly as you had hoped. During your regular prenatal care with the obstetrician, she will most likely tell you early on when to call her with your concerns. Ideally she will be agreeable and available anytime you have these worries and will encourage you to continue to call. If you need reassurance, here are the most common warnings we give patients about when to call and when to simply relax and continue to enjoy having your innards used for boxing practice, your esophagus for a toxic waste dump, and your skin for a scratching post.

The signs of labor and the subsequent instructions depend on how far you have gotten in your pregnancy. For most pregnancies term is defined as anytime after the thirty-seventh week. It is believed that after this time you and a baby would be safe if you were to deliver. While term pregnancy has not been defined differently for multiples, it is recognized that most multiple pregnancies will deliver before their due date. One-third of twin pregnancies will deliver before thirty-four weeks, and one-half by thirty-six weeks. Higher order multiples have higher risks due to those limitations mentioned in chapter 1.

One of the cardinal signs of labor is the presence of contractions. Your doctor and the nurses will badger you constantly about whether you feel them and will expect you to know without hesitation whether or not they are present. So the following is especially for the reader who is, as I was, a newbie when expecting multiples.

What Is a Contraction?

A contraction is a coordinated movement of the uterus designed to shrink its size and eventually help the cervix open and push the babies out of the body. It most often consists of contracting the smooth muscle of the wall of the uterus in a top-to-bottom or back-to-front motion. For most women it feels initially like a tightening in the belly that they first notice while rubbing (or scratching the skin off of) their bloated abdomens. As contractions become stronger, many women feel either abdominal or lower back discomfort that waxes and wanes in a somewhat regular fashion.

Just so you know, *men don't have contractions*. Don't expect your male OB to be able to explain what it feels like; the poor guy can only tell you what others have told him. If you aren't sure what to feel, ask a member of your sisterhood. They needn't have had multiples; if they've had kids and were not whisked through the convenience of a scheduled C-section or rendered unconscious by some turn of luck, they know how contractions feel.

A caveat is worthwhile here. Your sisters may seem too eager to help you understand the process of labor. There is a reason for this: A discussion of labor and delivery among women soon becomes the time-honored contest called "Who Had the Worst Time of It?" This is closely related to "My Kid's More Successful Than Your Kid" and "My Life Is Busier Than Your Life." It is one of the ways the female of the species determines the social pecking order. Here are the rules: The same mommies who have taught their babies to be kind to others choose the one in the group who has not yet given birth and haze her like a college freshman about how hard it is going to be.

The tournament often begins at the monthly bridge game or ladies' club meeting where the answer to the question "When are you due?" leads to contestant number one telling about the forty-eight-hour labor that ended when the doctor pulled the baby out with forceps without so much as a Tylenol, leaving her so torn that the doc couldn't put the pieces back together. It will continue to escalate until the triumphant one produces the C-section scar that hasn't healed in forty years. The expectant mom will dutifully leave the room to vomit, during which time the sisters will smile smugly at one another. It is the "ladies who lunch" version of what my mother calls a "pissing contest," and once you have delivered, you, too, may succumb to the temptation. And, hey, you'll win every time unless your group includes someone who has had more multiples than you. It would be kind to avoid frightening the uninitiated, but, then again, you didn't spare the poor plebe at school your senior year, either.

That said, if you're reading this, you have had your fill of ridiculous comments by others and need some info that actually helps you. What follows are directions concerning when to call the doctor's office for evaluation. If your doctor gives you different instructions, by all means follow them. Early detection of trouble can save your life—or those of your babies. You might consider tearing out this page or making a copy to post on your refrigerator.

The first order of business when these symptoms appear is *not to panic*. Lie down and rest. Get a large drink of water. Call your physician or the labor and delivery floor. Tell them your symptoms and await in-

Signs of Preterm Labor (earlier than thirty-eight weeks)

- Contractions that are ten minutes apart and regular for more than one hour
- Leaking of fluid of larger volume or of consistency different from normal discharge—even if you think it might be urine
- Vaginal bleeding, especially if it soaks more than one pad per hour

Signs of Term Labor (after thirty-eight weeks, if you're so lucky)

- Contractions are five minutes apart and regular for one hour
- Leaking of fluid of larger volume or of consistency different from normal discharge; again, even if you think it's nothing, call
- Vaginal bleeding, especially if it soaks more than one pad per hour

Signs of Other Potential Problems of Pregnancy

- Failure to feel your babies move for more than one hour at a time (although babies can sleep in ninety-minute cycles, so follow your doctor's advice on this one)
- Severe headaches, unlike the usual headaches you may have, that aren't relieved with rest or Tylenol
- Pains under the right breast below the rib cage that aren't related to the babies moving (a sign of hypertension and preeclampsia/eclampsia; see chapter 14)
- Swelling, especially of the face and hands and especially if it is sudden and you can't wear your jewelry

struction. If you are concerned that you are in labor, go ahead and go to the hospital. The rule of thumb many of us have been taught is that the average first-time mom will go to the hospital three times thinking she's in labor before she actually stays to have her baby—and that's when she expects only one. Believe me, your doctors and nurses will be much happier giving you reassurance and possibly sending you home than they will be trying to make up for lost time when someone waited too long so as not to "disturb" their caregivers. I felt silly every time I agreed to go to the hospital at my husband's urging and every time I ended up in the hospital for conditions that, left untreated, might have led to serious injury to my twins. Besides, you can always embellish enough to make each trip sound extra frightening for the next expectant mom you help initiate.

What to Expect During a Hospital Labor

Delivery in the hospital can take many forms depending on the circumstances of pregnancy. For women expecting multiples, it can vary from a multiple vaginal birth at full term to a scheduled or unscheduled cesarean section of sextuplets with twenty specialized medical personnel in attendance. Whatever your circumstance, the experience usually follows a pattern determined by the physicians who practice at the hospital, but some aspects are consistent enough for discussion here.

Preadmission/Preregistration: Before you anticipate needing to be in the hospital, it is usually recommended that you notify the hospital where you plan to deliver. This is an important step because not only does it allow time for your insurance company to learn that they will be shelling out money soon, but it also decreases how much of the six pounds of paperwork you will have to fill out in between the "she-she-she" part of your Lamaze breathing of active labor. You can do this step anytime during your pregnancy, but sooner is better since you may be there before you know it.

Admission: When you are sent to the hospital to deliver your babies, you will be admitted to the floor by the nursing staff. This usually consists of exchanging your clothes for a hospital gown, your nice jewelry for the plastic bracelet and abdominal belts (more about them in a minute), and your freedom for a nurse call light that you'll learn to press before you pee on yourself, so you can get help with the IV pole, those three or four belts, and the extra 20 pounds of fluid you just found around your ankles. In most circumstances you will be prohibited from eating or drinking anything until you deliver or until it is determined you are unlikely to deliver soon. The IV will be used to provide necessary medications and the fluids you aren't allowed to ingest on your own.

We often restrict a laboring woman's oral intake, especially of solid foods although not always of liquids, because of the perceived risk of her aspirating stomach contents into her lungs should she require a C-section. As bad as you've found the acid in your throat recently, it is better than the chemical burn or infection you could get in your lungs in this situation. When your friends with one baby tell you about their "natural" labor in which they ate a four-course meal, drank all they could of their favorite drinks, and still pushed out an eight-pounder without anesthetic, resist the urge to crush their windpipes. Remember their participation in the "pissing contest" and the likelihood that they are lying anyway since you know you haven't been able to eat even a slice of bread without getting gas.

What is all this stuff? The belts you have probably seen before, at your umpteenth nonstress test. One is used to measure the frequency of contractions and usually sits at the top of your uterus. The other belts will be for measuring each of your babies' heartbeats and will be placed anywhere on your torso, belly, or back to hear each and every one of them. I have no idea how those delivery nurses manage to find the heartbeats of four individual babies inside a two-by-two-foot space. They never cease to amaze me with their skill. The belts will be attached with cables to a monitor or monitors sitting beside your bed, and the data will be collected on a strip or strips of paper. The frequency and duration of your contractions will usually be printed on the bottom of the strip, and your babies' heartbeats recorded in a group at the top. You will be attached to these infernal restraints until every last baby is out of your body, and you will quickly learn the value of moisturizer: I have yet to see a monitor belt that doesn't make you itch like a fire ant pit.

Note to men and to well-meaning friends everywhere: It does *not* help the woman in labor to have you instruct her every five minutes that another contraction is coming. By the time you've noticed it, she can feel it, and she may hurt you if you keep it up. She can't help it; that's what animals do when they're in pain. If you're lucky and play your cards right, she will regain her sanity when this is all over and the triplets graduate college.

A special note about these strips: No matter what your husband says, he *cannot* tell that "this next contraction is gonna be a big one" because the strength of the contraction *cannot* be measured from the outside of your body. If he tells you this and insists on saying it over and over until you think you might pop him one as soon as you get through the next contraction, instead say, "That's nice, dear," and hand him this paragraph to read.

The Course of Labor—and That Delivery: Once you have been stripped naked and divested of the last shreds of your dignity, you enter labor. If your first baby is vertex, or head-down, and the babies are mature enough, you may be allowed to try to deliver vaginally. The contractions will become harder and closer together, the belts will itch, and the heartbeats on those monitors will thump-thump-thump until you reach the stage where you can push. If your situation does not allow you to deliver all the babies vaginally, you will be prepped for a C-section. The final outcome is dependent on your individual situation and the medical opinion of your OB.

If you must have a C-section, the upside may be that you can skip the fun of actual labor. If you are destined for the path I took, however, you can expect some or all of the following to happen before delivery:

1. *Early labor.* You have had contractions since the day you conceived, and with multiples you have felt them earlier than your sisters with single pregnancies, but contractions aren't labor until the cervix starts to thin and dilate. Early labor consists of light-to-moderate, usually irregular contractions and is associated with cervical dilation to four centimeters. This is the stage in which most of us live for weeks before we deliver,

and it's this stage that puts us at bed rest if our OBs find it necessary.

2. *Labor—first stage.* First, second, and third are the stages defined by a guy named Milton Friedman. The first stage includes the early labor above, called the "latent phase," during which the contractions become more regular and more forceful. It ends in the "active phase" when the cervix dilates to ten centimeters and you begin pushing.
3. *Labor—second stage.* This stage starts when you begin pushing unless by now you have been diverted to the surgical track. It won't end until all those darlings are out of your body.
4. *Labor—third stage.* After the babies come out, you still have to deliver the placenta or placentas. That is why it is called the "afterbirth."

Sometime during this process you will recall your earlier fears about just how much pain you may have to endure. Before you approach the final hurrah, you will be asked what, if anything, you'd like to do for pain control. Superwoman will, of course, ask what is best for the babies and insist on bearing her discomfort for the greater good of the whole. Those of us lower on the chain of superiority will already have lost our minds, strangled our husbands, and threatened the staff within an inch of their lives if they stick us one more time. So what is a well-meaning but psychotic mom-to-be in labor to do?

Anesthesia, God's Gift to Laboring Women

In my obstetric practice I talk to my patients about what we know about pain control and its effects on mom and baby. I advocate for delivery without epidural anesthesia because of some evidence that epidurals increase the chance of operative delivery, including C-section, forceps, and vacuum extraction. Additionally, I tell them that elevated temperatures, often otherwise a sign of infection in a newborn, can be due to epidurals and increase the risk of unnecessary intervention on the baby. However, I also tell them that despite the above statement, long-term ill effects on babies due to their moms having had epidurals have not been shown. After a discussion of the risks and the benefits, I let moms choose. Nine times out of ten they have the epidural once they are in active labor.

Why? Let's face it: Labor hurts. We all know the jokes about "that's why they call it labor" (usually told by men who will never have the pleasure), so I'll skip them. Pushing a 4-inch head through a one-inch hole is not pleasant. Pushing the pelvis out of joint to get that self-same head through the canal is not pleasant. Feeling every last stitch if the doctor has to sew our sensitive parts back together just flat-out hurts.

Epidurals work, but they are not the only option available. Spinal anesthesia, saddle blocks, local blocks, and intravenous narcotics help. So do some nonpharmacologic choices such as massage, warm water, cutaneous nerve stimulation, position change, acupressure, acupuncture, and sterile water injection. There are lots of resources available that discuss these "alternative" therapies for labor pain, and I suggest you look into them and perhaps try some or all in early labor if your doctor deems it safe. I've included a few resources for these alternative approaches in the Resources section. Most women who are expecting multiples will require some sort of anesthesia because many will end up with a C-section.

The pharmacologic (using medicines) methods of controlling labor pain are as follows:

Intravenous Narcotics: Most often used in the first portion of labor, intravenous narcotics decrease but do not take away the pain. They do help one not to care about the pain quite so much. We use several drugs. Depending on the tradition in your part of the country, you may receive Demerol, Stadol, or other medicines, including morphine. Morphine is also used to stop ineffective or preterm labor if other measures have failed. My best night's sleep in several months came during labor when my OB gave me morphine; I will love the man until the day I die for giving me those four hours of bliss. The downside of these medicines is their effect on Mom's and babies' systems. As they make Mom sleepy (to the point that she could stop breathing if she gets too much), so, too, do they make babies sleepy (and sleepy babies don't want to breathe, either—a problem once the cord is cut). We don't often use these drugs after the first stage of labor for this reason.

Saddle and Local Blocks: These are injections of numbing medicine to different sites near or in the vagina. One is designed to block all sensation to the whole region of pelvic skin called the perineum and is injected into a nerve in the pelvis through the vagina. The other is injected into the outer skin itself and blocks sensation at the exit from the birth canal to help with the pain from skin tearing or an episiotomy if it is needed. Both must be done soon before birth and do not help with abdominal or back pain. Neither has much effect on the babies directly, but each has the potential for the needle injuring—or the medicine being injected into—a baby should anyone move unexpectedly.

Epidural and Spinal Anesthesia: These are the "gold standard" for control of labor pain and consist of an injection into the spine of the pregnant woman. An epidural usually involves the placement of a small tube (catheter) into Mom's back just outside the dura mater, a membrane that contains and protects the spinal cord. A constant supply of anesthetic is infused through this catheter, and it can be increased or decreased depending on the desired effect. A spinal block is a onetime injection placed a bit more superficially and without the ability for continuous infusion. Both types are intended to numb the entire body below the point of injection. Both types have a risk for infection or bleeding at the point of the needle's entry and for causing numbness of the diaphragm, the primary muscle of breathing located just under the rib cage. The bleeding can often cause a "spinal headache," a nasty bugger that is sometimes difficult to control without a further procedure. Numbing the diaphragm is obviously a bad thing since a person doesn't breathe too well without breathing muscles. Other problems can occur with this type of pain control, as they can anytime someone enters your body with a foreign object, but usually it goes off without a hitch.

Postscript 2003

After years of my mother telling me about her two labors with no pain control, I thought I had to do it the way she did it to be a "real woman." Again with the hazing! Besides, I tell women not to have epidurals. But when I learned I would be delivering twins, I immediately wanted an epidural because I didn't want my OB to have to wait to slice me open at the first sign of trouble. I figured it would be worth the appearance of a loss of professional integrity to have two healthy babies even if it made me less of a woman in Mom's eyes.

After I delivered, I shared these thoughts with my mom, who said that the only reason she had no anesthesia was that the only thing available was "twilight sleep" (a combination of scopolamine and morphine), which she translated as "behave like a mental patient, feel every twinge, remember nothing." She said she would have had an epidural in a heartbeat. Maybe when it comes right down to it, the presence of a "pissing contest" is in the eye of the beholder.

The Blessed Event: Vaginal or C-Section?

Whether you deliver vaginally or are slit sideways or up and down is dependent on many factors. If the babies are old enough, and usually only if they each present headfirst, you may be allowed to try to deliver on your own. If the first baby is head-down but the others are butt first, the doctor may let you deliver anyway or may try a maneuver called external version, in which he tries to rotate the baby by firmly massaging the outside of your body. Having failed to deliver all babies vaginally, he can always switch to the C-section as his backup. The approach he chooses will depend in large part on the standards set in your community, the maturity and size of the babies, and your OB's comfort level with your ability to be successful at a vaginal delivery. The variables that are factored into your OB's decision-making process are too many and more complex than can be handled within the scope of this book, but a few approaches are mentioned here.

Should the OB believe you need a C-section, you will be moved into a surgical room (if you weren't already there) and your belly prepped with brown soap called Betadine. Your body will be covered with sterile drapes, and a tray full of equipment that looks as if it is straight out of a dungeon will be pulled close to you. During this time your OB will tell jokes or ask you seemingly meaningless questions to which you think he should already know the answer. You may see the anesthesiologist nod and grin during this episode; he's the only one outside of perhaps your husband that you can see directly. He and the OB are engaging in a secret ritual during which the OB has been poking you with needles and pinching your skin within an inch of its life, and the anesthesiologist has been telling him that you feel no pain. Once the OB is convinced you won't hurt, he begins to cut.

I will spare you the details since you may already be nauseous enough, what with the babies playing jai alai while you try to read. The thing to note is that if the OB thinks the babies will turn out well, you may prefer that he cut you *transversely*, or in a horizontal fashion, rather than vertically. A vertical incision may be necessary to reduce the risk of injury to very premature babies, but the transverse incision is generally preferred because you will be at a somewhat lower risk of your uterus rupturing during the course of another pregnancy should you lose your mind and decide you ever want to try this again.

During the course of delivery, whether vaginal or cesarean, you will realize that you haven't yet lost all your dignity during the admissions process. With the vaginal delivery comes the time when you push until you pass gas on the doctor, pee on yourself, and soil yourself and others. Doctors are used to this: Don't worry about apologizing; it's part of why they get the big bucks. The doc will just clean you up and will most likely say nothing about it. During a C-section (and sometimes during a vaginal birth), you will most likely end up vomiting from the pressure in your abdomen right before you feel the glorious release of your lungs to take their first deep breath in many months.

You will get through this process, and the babies will be born. Lord willing, they will all be healthy and able to survive with various needs for support by the medical staff. Most likely they will be taken to the NICU, if only for observation, and you will be cleaned and made more comfortable. When you are able, you will be allowed to meet them all for the first time.

There is one circumstance of your delivery that is different from that of your friends who had only one baby each: More likely than not, you will be rooming separately from your babies and leaving without them. It is a bittersweet moment when you realize you are not like the other moms and will never be. Despite all your fears at this time, try to rejoice in it. Remember what Mom said: This, too, shall pass, and in the meantime you have an opportunity that other moms do not. You can savor the added time you have been allowed for transition between being pregnant and being a mom. Whether the transition time lasts days or weeks, you must take the time to celebrate your achievement and your babies' arrival in this world. You will be buying bigger and better baby gates soon enough.

PART 3

Receiving the Storks

Ten

Remembering to Celebrate

March 7, 2001

Emma and Jack are born, and I can breathe again! I'm so worried about them. Emma is okay so far but breathing heavily, and Jack has had to be given surfactant and put on the ventilator. I'm lucky in that I really trust these people, since they are partly responsible for my training and since they tell me the babies will be okay. I am trying to believe them.

I had decided early in the pregnancy that I wanted to take a break and celebrate with my family when the babies were born. The only craving I had the whole time I was pregnant was for soft white French cheese, grapes, and a baguette, and I knew I couldn't have the cheese. Ben and I smuggled a bottle of champagne into the hospital in my bag. We figured if this doesn't deserve champagne, nothing does. Dad was so kind. He drove all over town after I delivered to find the bread, cheese, and grapes, and even bought a case of champagne glasses at the local discount store.

We popped open the bottle in front of everyone and started offering glasses—even just sips—to anyone who walked in the door. Two friends from church stopped by to see how I was doing and shared a glass with us. Even the nurses—who shall remain nameless—had a sip. I ate bread and cheese until I was nearly sick. I had no heartburn. And I had fun.

For the first time in a long time, I feel like a part of my community again.

Congratulations! You have survived fatigue, nausea, aches, pains, itching, swelling, contractions, shortness of breath, heartburn, preterm labor, and bed rest. You may also be a survivor of gestational diabetes, preeclampsia, hypertension, hyperemesis, and a host of other ills of your pregnancy. Your prize? Children! Fabulous, wonderful children who will soon enough be soiling your clothes, soiling their clothes, crying at 3:00 a.m. (and 4:00 and 6:00 and 8:30), and trying by any means necessary to test the outer limits of your energy, aptitude, and abilities in order to spot and exploit your weaknesses later. Until that time you have a very narrow window of opportunity during which you can remain your own person. You are able to rest when you wish and eat when you wish, talk when you wish and to whom you wish—all without the pants-cuff pull of ankle-biters jealous for your attention.

Now is the time to party. You will never again have the same chance to be yourself. Above all, once the babies are all home, you will never again have the same uninterrupted time to sit down and celebrate your accomplishment. This is when you can pay attention to yourself again—heaven knows you've earned it. You have spent the last months giving every last bit of energy to making the healthiest babies you could make, and you will spend the rest of your life supporting these babies' rise to adulthood and worrying about them.

How to Host a Party in a Hospital

A hospital environment may seem like the last place to throw a party. It's cold, it's sterile, and it's full of people you don't know poking and prodding you every four hours. On the other hand, someone else will be cleaning up the mess. By "party" I mean more than an entertainment event involving invited guests and your best silver, although I encourage you to have that experience if you wish. I mean that even during your recovery from the delivery, you need to begin to establish a mind-set of celebration and thanksgiving and to encourage the development of that mind-set in those around you.

The first thing is to recognize that you deserve this party. It is the celebration of you and your babies, and of everyone's survival of the ordeal you've been through. Even if one or more of the babies are in trouble or you are concerned about their health, you are all survivors of this stage of life. Go ahead: Call your friends and family. Tell them the news. Then unplug the phone, log on to your laptop, and send a few video e-mails to your address book. Let your husband set up a Web site if that is what he wants to do. We sent (and posted on a temporary Web site) videos of the babies even while they were on ventilators and under oxygen hoods with tubes in their noses. By spreading the good news you can begin to realize that despite the circumstances of your delivery, the very fact that you have delivered these children is indeed a good thing.

The second thing is to go through the motions of a person who is celebrating. You have begun by spreading the good news. Next, actually celebrate the good news with a small get-together as soon as you are allowed to eat. Think about what it is you have most craved during your pregnancy that you either could not have or could not tolerate. Don't settle for a take-out pizza or hospital food for your party unless you must. You don't need to spend much money, but you should be sure to have what makes you feel that you are really treating yourself. It will reinforce in your psyche that something good has happened, and it will ease the shock of the reality of your motherhood and the burden of worry about the babies' health, even if only temporarily.

Enlist the help of those who can leave the hospital for this—you're a bit busy during labor. Most of us know beforehand who will be around when we deliver. Find a grandparent or friend who is looking for a way to help and give her a shopping list or make him the delivery person to your favorite restaurant. Be specific: Almost anyone who takes this task will do his or her best to fill the bill exactly as you request. Then, while you focus on getting your babies healthily into the world, your loved ones will be catering the after-party.

As you celebrate, include the nursing staff and others who come into the room to check on you. It's a great way to let them know you're grateful for all they do to help you and your children pass through this episode safely. It won't hurt the level of attention you receive, either. Most people do their best to do their jobs well, and it is especially easy for nursing staff and other hospital employees to feel put-upon and disrespected. By asking them to join you, you recognize them and the work they do, and the mind-set you are trying to establish will filter through their days and on to the next patients for whom they care.

The third thing after recognizing your right to party and actually having the celebration is to record it for your memory and for your children. Even if they are healthy enough to be allowed to stay in the room with you and will be going home with you, they will not remember how people acted when they were born. Take lots of photos. A video is even better, especially if you and your loved ones record welcome messages to the babies. Write your thoughts in the journal. All babies have special circumstances that surround their births, and we all need reassurance that we were truly wanted and loved when we came into the world. When one of your children despairs that she was ever born—about the same time that she gets her first zit—it can be helpful to have available the welcome video or Mom's journal to remind her of her worth. It can boost your mind-set of celebration when it flags under the stress of caring for well or ill babies or threatens to turn from simple baby blues into a more serious depressive condition.

What if You Can't Party: Baby Blues and Postpartum Depression

Once the blessed event has passed and you have delivered your babies by whatever means necessary, you may look at your husband and wonder if you did something he's angry about, and you may listen or look for your babies and see if they're all right. Everyone in the room will be watching for you to have certain emotions based on their own preconceived notions of what a new mom is supposed to feel. Forget the onlookers for a moment. You may feel anything from fear to joy to love to apathy to thankfulness to confusion. No emotion is wrong to have initially, and you've earned the right to feel however you happen to feel at this time.

One of the most common feelings a new mom can have, even with a normal delivery of a single healthy baby, is a sense of disconnectedness or even disappointment. These are called the "baby blues," a time when you may feel guilty for not being elated, feel confused because you aren't thrilled, and question why you did any of this in the first place because you don't feel as you expected to feel. You may even cry a little without being able to control it. All of these are normal feelings right after delivery and are part of the transition from pregnant woman to mom.

Take a moment to pause and consider the facts. You have been through the most difficult ordeal of your life, and you are exhausted. You have had many months to establish detailed expectations of how events would pass and how you would feel (and possibly additional years of dreaming about pregnancy), and the reality may have been very different. You need a few days of adjustment time to resolve this. There is also the physical reality of staring into the mirror after your first opportunity to bathe and seeing your misshapen mass of a deflated abdomen that feels like crepe paper and wondering if you will ever again look or feel normal. There is the emotional reality of looking at a newborn and realizing not that it is a cute little baby but that it is your offspring and that your life as you know it has changed forever. To those facts add the major hormonal shifts that occur in the first few days after delivery, and you have found yourself in the worst case of PMS you have ever experienced—all while those around you are conducting themselves like blithering idiots, cooing and fawning over you and the babies. It is a wonder more of us aren't carted off to the asylum right after giving birth, and kept in locked rooms until our children are grown.

These "baby blues" are considered normal and are temporary, affecting more than half of us within the first three or four days and usually ending within the first ten days after delivery. It is during this time that the measures above intended to teach us again how to party will help us reconnect with ourselves and our families, and allow us to find the joy in our newfound parenthood. We reassure ourselves that we will again exercise and eat properly, and we will find ourselves back in our old shape within a year, barring new health problems brought by the pregnancy. We learn to accept the change in the priorities of our lives, recognizing that this parental responsibility is precisely what we had agreed to when we decided we wanted to become parents. The hormonal shifts begin to balance themselves out, and over time we regain our sanity and renew the determination to face the challenges of this life. We once again become whole people, simply changed forever by the experience of childbirth and parenting.

Unfortunately, up to one in ten of us will progress from the "baby blues" into true postpartum depression (PPD). PPD begins anytime from the first twenty-four hours after delivery to months later, and it can last for months or up to two years before being diagnosed and treated or eventually resolving. Considerably underdiagnosed, it is a true medical illness that, if left untreated, can progress to chronic depression and even to psychotic behavior, including suicide and murder, as has been in evidence too often in the media. Even in situations involving PPD that do not end tragically, the effects on the family are profound. Marriages suffer. Extended families often withdraw, uncertain how to help. Babies as young as three months recognize the symptoms in their mothers and have been shown to react to her change in mood by modifying their behavior, which is important because children's personalities are shaped in this early stage of development. Studies have shown that babies born to and raised by mothers with PPD have problems with cognitive ability, language development, and attention (meaning they have demonstrated in these studies a lack of ability to concentrate as intently as other babies, not necessarily that they get attention deficit disorder from having moms with PPD).

The symptoms of PPD can go unrecognized because many mirror the normal changes a woman experiences during the transition from pregnancy to parenthood, because she fails to keep follow-up appointments with her doctor (or has none scheduled), because she or her family do not want to accept that depression is a medical illness that requires treatment, or because of a number of other social or societal factors. Other medical illnesses (anemia or thyroid problems, for example) also often mask or imitate the symptoms of PPD.

Postpartum depression is defined by the presence of some or all of the following symptoms:

1. Feelings of sadness
2. Loss of interest or pleasure in activities
3. Irritability and agitation
4. Feelings of worthlessness or guilt
5. Weight loss
6. Loss of energy
7. Sleeping problems (trouble sleeping or sleeping too much)
8. Loss of concentration
9. Inability to make decisions
10. Frequent thoughts of death or suicide

Clearly, some of these symptoms can happen just by being a new mom, and this sometimes confuses the diagnosis until the more serious symptoms appear. Most at risk for postpartum depression are women who have previously battled depression or a prior episode of postpartum depression, those whose pregnancy was more stressful than they had expected (and we with multiples fit right in there), and those who are unhappy with their relationship to their partner or who feel unloved and under- or unsupported during their ordeal.

The important items to note here are that PPD is a true medical illness to be taken seriously and evaluated when symptoms are present and that PPD can be successfully treated. Treatment initially consists of counseling, both for the affected woman and for her partner, with the focus being on interpersonal relationships, the nature of the woman's changing role in life, and the education of the partner in how he can be supportive and find his own support. There is some debate about the nature of hormone replacement therapy due to recognition of our sensitivity to hormone fluctuations during this time. Initial studies have suggested there may be some benefit to the use of estrogen replacement, but the potential dangers of extra estrogen in a woman recovering from pregnancy require that more studies be done before this can be recommended.

All this leaves us with medications for treatment of depression. Very little is known about the effects of antidepressants in breast-feeding women; although we know that antidepressants are found in breast milk, we do not have definitive evidence of their long-term effects in babies. Since some studies have shown no ill effects and some have shown an increase in irritability in babies who have been exposed, we therefore use caution when discussing medical treatment of PPD in breast-feeding moms. Often, counseling and frequent follow-up with their doctor is all women with PPD need. Sometimes, however, PPD can hang on too long or be so severe that women have trouble caring for themselves or their children. In this circumstance we believe the benefit of treatment outweighs the risks of treatment, and we discuss this with the patient and her partner.

The most common medications used have been the tricyclic antidepressants Elavil, Pamelor, and Tofranil, which are among the oldest and for which we have the most long-term safety data. More and more we are beginning to use the SSRIs—Prozac, Zoloft, and Luvox have been studied for PPD specifically—because of their lower risk of side effects and their ability to be taken only once daily. The duration of treatment remains under discussion, but current thinking is that women with PPD who require medication should continue treatment for about twelve months from the time they feel normal again. Women who have a relapse of symptoms will need to restart medication and continue for longer periods of time.

After you have delivered your multiples, if you feel emotional highs or lows that seem out of proportion to the way you believe you should feel, by all means mention them to your OB before you are sent home (or call at the onset of such feelings if you are already at home). Ask her to schedule a follow-up visit in her office within two weeks so she can reassess your health and your mood, and monitor you for the development of PPD. If you should feel suicidal or have fantasies or thoughts of harming your babies, call her immediately and ask for the number of a psychiatrist who can help you. Most important, do not ignore the warning signs of PPD. You deserve to feel better if you have it, and those babies need you at your best in order to thrive in their new world, especially if their new world is the intensive care unit.

Eleven

The NICU

March 7, 2001

Went to see the babies in the NICU for the first time. It's so strange to see them separated after spending their whole lives together. Jack did well initially but had to be put on the ventilator to help him breathe. Funny, I feel less afraid about him than I do about watching Emma continue to fight under the oxy hood. They both have IVs now and feeding tubes in their noses, and I look at them and feel . . . disconnected.

Is it because they are here in this foreign and sterile environment and not in the room with me that I feel this way? Am I preventing myself from being overwhelmed by fear or sadness by using my "doctor mode" to see them as mere patients? I thought childbirth was supposed to be wonderful. I expected to have that unbounded joy when I first saw them. Is it because I'm afraid for them that I can't rejoice?

March 14, 2001

Why won't this baby eat? They're so small—Emma has dropped to just under five pounds; Jack is holding his own at four. I've cared for "feeder-growers" before, and I know I'm supposed to know that preemies just have to learn to eat. But I can't take them home until they've eaten enough, and I only have thirty minutes each time to try, or they start burning more calories trying to eat than they get through the milk. Jack's doing all right, but Emma will hardly try. I feel as if everyone is watching us fail in our first test of parenthood. The neonatologist tried to make me feel better by stating his opinion that perhaps she should have been on the ventilator, too; she just fought so hard to breathe that she ran out of energy to eat. Even so, I feel as if I'm never going to get to take her home!

Postscript 2003

We found out that Emma just likes taking her own sweet time to eat. . . . It's remarkable what hindsight offers.

So you've completed your pregnancy and delivered two or more beautiful babies. Unless you've been extremely fortunate, your kids have been whisked off to a foreign place filled with awesome mysteries and a few fears. Your challenge—and you must accept it, no choice here—is to help your babies find the path from here to their home with you while maintaining your health and your sanity. This is no simple task, but luckily for you, many others have trod the road before you, and an understanding of the workings of the place, when combined with a sense of humor, can help you, too, survive the NICU. Consider what follows as a "rough guide" to surviving the NICU. If you would like specific details regarding certain illnesses that babies may face here, go to the Rapid Reference Guide in chapter 15.

What Is All This Stuff?

If you or your partner consider yourselves gadget fanatics, there is no place like an intensive care unit of a major hospital to stoke the flames of desire to play, prod, or test the equipment. Unfortunately, if you've been allowed inside the inner sanctum of technology that is an NICU, it's probably because you have a baby inside one receiving care. You will probably fit into one of two categories in this place. Either you will be so consumed with concern for the welfare of your little ones that your will to play has faded altogether, or (more likely) you will be reassured by the stability of your babies' conditions but will be afraid (and rightly so) of breaking something.

An NICU has gizmos aplenty; they whir, they chirp, they buzz. Lights flash, tubes puff, and hoses suck and gurgle. An eerie blue light, not unlike the light of dusk, glows faintly from an adjoining space, bathing babies with goggles like girls in tanning beds. Tiny bags of juices of various colors carefully placed on poles drip in and out of tiny bodies. It is the bodies of *your* babies you will worry about, and you'll find yourself wondering, "What are they doing with all this stuff?"

When they are first born, your twins or more will be given a thorough once-over, and, after appropriate efforts are made to be sure they're stable, they will receive their first pieces of jewelry. The first *bijoux* are their ankle and wrist bracelets, used to identify them as yours. Next will come a silver or gold pendant, usually heart-shaped, placed on the babies' chests or backs. This medallion will be used to monitor your babies' body temperature, and it is important because a drop in temperature can cause problems for newborns, especially preemies. So far these trinkets are not available at Tiffany's, but I'm sure that someone, somewhere is thinking of a way to make heirlooms out of them and sell them on eBay.

Let's look first at the equipment used to keep your babies comfortable. Your babies will likely be taken with their jewelry and placed either in an infant warmer or an incubator cabinet. Which is used will depend in large part on the age and health of your babies when they're born. The warmer, heated from above by lamps, with four short sides and open to the air, is used most commonly. It helps older babies keep warm after birth and is used when it is anticipated that babies will soon be able to control their own body temperature. It is also used in the early stages of infant support (called resuscitation) when doctors and nurses are working with the babies to be sure they can breathe and have strong heartbeats. This machine has controls to measure the babies' body temperatures and to adjust the lamps to keep the babies' temps within range. The openness of the warmer allows easy access for babies to receive fluids if necessary and for the placement of the bili lights (see below). Later your babies will move from here to a regular crib, hopefully the last bed they'll know before their own at home.

The incubator-type warmer is closed to the outside environment and is used for infants of younger age. These babies may not yet be able to regulate their body temperatures or control the loss of moisture from their bodies. The incubators prevent drafts, limit exposure to some illnesses that other babies in the NICU may be fighting, conserve or add moisture to the infants' environment, and may provide ready-made tanning beds for the bathing beauties (see jaundice in chapter 15). The incubators provide access to your babies through holes in the side through which your hands—with or without gloves—can pass to touch them. More knobs and buttons exist on this type of bed than the others; they regulate temperature, moisture, and light.

Once doctors get your babies comfortable, they monitor their body functions. At the sides of each baby's crib you will find the most fun gadgets. The one that is vying for your attention with its insistent beeps, squiggly lines, and rapidly changing number display goes by a variety of names. It is often called simply "the Machine." The Machine monitors blood pressure, pulse, respiratory rate, and the amount of oxygen in each baby's blood. It may also provide a readout of the electrical activity of each baby's heart. It will perform these tasks continuously to provide a real-time update of your babies' condition to their caregivers. Many of these functions are transmitted through that medallion each baby is wearing on his or her torso.

The first and last word about the Machine is this: If it squeals—and it will—*don't panic!* The first rule we teach medical students about the Machine—any machine—is to treat the Patient, not the Machine. Your babies may be in trouble if the Machine squawks, and the nursing staff will not ignore it, but most likely the babies will be sleeping soundly and have just dislodged some piece of monitoring equipment that the Machine needs to feel secure in its value as the Machine.

Next we turn to those pieces of equipment used to support the babies' body functions. The runner-up to the Machine in the category "most likely to annoy and strike fear in a new parent" is the ventilator. It is second only because unlike the Machine, it is not used on every single baby in the NICU. The ventilator is a larger box than the Machine and often sits on the opposite side of the bed from it. The ventilator is used to provide respiratory support to babies who are too weak or too young to breathe on their own, and when it howls, people jump, although, again, we treat the patient and not the machine. If you happen to be in the NICU when alarms go off, try to remain calm. Babies frequently dislodge their breathing tubes, and this is an appropriate cause for concern. Nurses will check your baby's airway and, if necessary, provide the intervention to continue to support his breathing until the tube can be put back in place. However, if it is simply the Machine or the ventilator that is having a problem, the tantrum of beeping will soon be calmed, and everyone can go about his or her life again.

There is other equipment that wishes it had the intimidating muscles of the Machine and the ventilator, but while they are important, most are not as impressive. There are the bili lights, used to help babies break down their bilirubin (yellow blood pigment, see chapter 15) into a form that is removed from their bodies through their bowel movements; the vent hood (or oxy hood or whatever "hood" your NICU calls it), used to provide extra oxygen to babies who need it but do not require the assistance of the ventilator; and the IV equipment, essential for giving babies nutrition, blood, fluid, antibiotics, and other lifesaving interventions, but able to manage only a weak bleat when a problem arises.

Lots more equipment exists in the NICU, but many—such as diapers—are self-explanatory. (Did you know that nurses sometimes actually weigh those things to see how much fluid your babies produce?) Others have a specialized purpose you can ask the nurse about. (That bag on my boy's wee-wee is for what again?)

Who Are All These People Touching My Babies?

A variety of people will be caring for your babies every day. At the beginning of each shift your little ones will be assigned to a nurse or nurses. Most NICUs try to limit the number of infants their nurses care for to somewhere from a single critically ill baby to three "feeder growers" (see chapter 15). Many NICUs go to the trouble of assigning the same nurse to the same patients every day. This is designed to improve the continuity of care from day to day, allowing the nurse's skilled eyes to detect subtle changes in your babies' conditions over time.

For the most part these professionals are RNs with special training in pediatrics and/or ICU care of infants. Although their high level of knowledge and skill can be intimidating, most of them are eager to calm fears and explain procedures. They can also be the best advocates other than parents that a newborn could have. While reminding me that in the NICU I was "just another mom, not a doctor" (reassuring because I didn't have the pressure of maintaining appearances), our twins' nurses helped us deal with the frustrations of preemie development and complications, and helped us argue for "co-sleeping" the babies, to be discussed later.

Rely on the nurses' experience. Ask them what is happening and what will happen next. If you're having trouble, ask them what would be the best way to approach the doctor with questions. Those who have been there long enough can provide very helpful insights into what to expect and can allay some of your fears.

Other members of the health care team include respiratory therapists, or RTs. These people smooth over the feelings of the ventilator, keeping it running properly. They administer treatments to keep babies' lungs working well and monitor the delivery of oxygen to babies and to the machines that serve them.

Dieticians and nutritionists provide the doctors with guidance about the proper ingredients in nutritional formulas to support growth and development of these young bodies in their care. Physical or occupational therapists may stop by on occasion to assess your babies' potential needs for programs in the hospital or at home to help them catch up developmentally to their cohorts (other babies born at the same time they were) or to provide treatment for disabilities they may have. Radiology technicians will be taking X-rays and doing ultrasounds when the doctor requests it to assess your babies' health.

If that sounds like an awful lot of people touching your babies, it is. However, they all work together to assure that your newborns' experience in the NICU is as short and as comfortable as possible and that they come out of the NICU as healthy, happy newborns.

So What Can I Do in Here?

As mentioned earlier, it is not a good idea to try to reprogram the equipment in the NICU. However, that is not to say that you should stay out or sit idly by while others "do things" to those babies you have worked so hard to get this far. No matter how prematurely born or how ill they are, you can always do something.

Love the babies. No matter how young they are, your babies were born knowing the sound of your voice and the warmth of your body. The hospital staff is dedicated to caring for their health, but no one can comfort your children the way you can. If they are too young to hold, stand by their incubator and sing to them (unless you sound like a dying frog; there are other ears listening, you know). Talk to them and tell them how much you love them, how you can't wait to bring them home, how well they're doing. If they are able, practice Kangaroo Care (a method in which a baby is swaddled close to a parent with the baby's naked skin touching the parent's naked skin in a quiet environment, shown to improve growth and health parameters in premature NICU babies) or hold them while they eat—as often as you can during the day.

Be good to yourself. Your babies need you, but they won't be comforted by parents who are too stressed to see them or are so agitated or tired when they see them that they can't follow any advice. Babies know our emotions and respond to them from an early age; our irritability may very well rub off on them and delay their ability to go home with us, as was discussed in the previous chapter.

Remember that you just completed what will perhaps be the most grueling time of your life, both physically and mentally. You need rest, and you need quiet time to reconnect with your partner and begin your recovery. To that end, you might be enticed to see your children's sojourn in the NICU as a vacation for you as a couple before delving into 24/7 parenthood.

Don't beat yourself up for feeling this way. The lady in the adjacent delivery room who had only one baby doesn't get the same luxury. Use the time you are not at the NICU to take those naps you had so wished you could take when you were too uncomfortable to do so. Have an evening with your partner at a nice restaurant, celebrating the event of your children's birth, and remind yourself that you are owed this for the work you've done. This will be the only time you have to remember that you are a couple first and that the babies are an extension of your lives together. Cherish it.

Breast-feed the babies (if possible). Every baby does best with breast milk. There is evidence that suggests that a woman's body makes just the right kind of milk for her own baby's stage of development, whether for preemies' immature intestines or for a baby born at full term. You may not be able to get your babies to nurse, but that should not be a barrier to their obtaining the healthiest food for their developing bodies. Only in unusual circumstances is a new mom not able to make adequate milk if she is motivated to do so.

Every hospital has a specialized nurse called a lactation consultant whose responsibility is to teach every willing new mother to breast-feed her babies. For those whose infants can't nurse yet, she can get you started with a breast pump. Expect it to take a good three to five days to have a quality output with each session, but give every last drop you make to the NICU nurses. They won't laugh at you and will be kind enough to give it to your children if the babies can eat. That first milk contains powerful immune system factors that protect your babies as only you can.

> In the first two days I used the pump, I got a solid four or five drops at each session. By the time my twins were two months old, I could make eight to ten ounces per session. Talk about a weight loss plan—I was burning almost 1,800 calories per day just sitting and making milk!

If your babies are old enough to learn to nurse (around thirty-six weeks) but can't yet leave the NICU, have the nurses set aside a quiet room or, at minimum, a privacy screen. Most NICUs already have a place to assist mothers who want to breast-feed. You may need the patience of Job to ignore the Machine and the exhibitionist tendencies of a porn star to expose your breasts to potentially the whole world, but think of it as practice for the time you try to get dressed after your shower while the two-year-olds are pulling at your naked legs and yelling, "Eat! Eat!"

For more details on breast-feeding resources, see the Resources section. One book I recommend highly is *The Complete Book of Breastfeeding* by Marvin S. Eiger, M.D., and Sally Wendkos Olds (see Resources), which also contains advice about preemie feeding.

Advocate for the babies. Okay, so you're not an expert on the care and feeding of newborns, much less preemies or sick infants. By no means let that be an excuse not to be educated about their progress, aware of plans for their care, or enthusiastic in your desire to comfort and protect them.

Talk to other parents of NICU babies (they will be volunteered to you the moment you tell a soul you have one in the hospital). Ask them what issues they faced in their babies' care and what, in retrospect, they wished they had seen done for their babies. At minimum you will want to know from the nurses each day when the doctor saw them, what each requires to be discharged from the hospital, and what is planned for that day to help them get there.

One way you can advocate for your babies is by asking the doctor and nurses about "co-sleeping," a situation in which your babies share the same crib. Studies have shown that co-sleeping multiples in the NICU improves each baby's blood oxygen content, growth, and feeding. By sharing body heat they can conserve energy for these other tasks, and it is my opinion that your babies, who have been together their entire lives before birth, know when another is near or gone and that they are capable of missing one another even at such young ages. If they are too young or frail, or equipment needs require it, they may need to remain apart for a time, but I found that in the NICU where my children were, the question had simply never come up. The doctors and nurses agreed it was good for them, but the hospital administration initially refused, citing a lack of protocol. We had the protocol from Children's Hospital just across the street faxed to the administrator, and our twins were co-sleeping the next day and every day thereafter. To this day, as they sleep in their shared bed, two-year-old Jack strokes his sister's head.

What Do You Mean I Get to Take Only One Home Today?

Like it or not, your babies will probably come home the way they came out—one at a time. The reunion of the family as a whole unit may take days, weeks, or months depending on the needs of each baby. You are now left with some difficult priorities. If you are the milk cow sustaining the babies, you will be pumping for one while nursing or pumping for the other every three hours, and the babies may be hundreds of miles apart depending on where you live in relation to the hospital where you delivered. If you live close, you will still need to be sure you spend time caring for those at home while loving and advocating for those in the NICU. If you have other children at home, you've already been dealing with this problem, but for the new parent it comes as a shock once the exodus begins.

There will be plenty of opportunities for hyperventilating over your worries. Remember that your first fainting spell likely came the time you first saw the ultrasound picture of your multiples inside you. Recall how you learned to accept the reality and conquer your initial fears. Choose now to step back and focus on your options, and remember the old saw that what doesn't kill us strengthens us. You can do this, too.

Your first and most pressing issue is finding a way to be as close geographically to each baby as is practical. If you live many miles away, ask the NICU nurses to call a social worker and ask her if facilities exist where you might stay with the baby you have near those still in the hospital. Most large hospitals have a Ronald McDonald House or other place nearby designed as a short-term "home" for those with

If you breast-feed or pump, consider this sample schedule: Every three hours or so you feed the baby who is with you. If you are breast-feeding and have help, feed the baby from one breast while pumping with the other, since milk will be leaking from the other breast anyway. If you would rather wait or are bottle-feeding your pumped milk, feed the baby and let your helper change his diaper and burp him while you pump for the other. After storing the milk and cleaning the equipment, you can then play with the baby you have. The whole process will initially take up to an hour each time (again, it takes a motivated mom!), but after a while you will be able to feed, diaper, pump, and be ready to play or nap in about thirty minutes each time with twins. The process will take longer the more babies you have, and you will definitely need more help for triplets or more.

family members in the hospital. Some hospitals have empty wings that were once used for patient care but have been modified for short-stay needs. If no such places are available, contact a local congregation of your religious faith. Explain to them your situation and ask for help. You may be able to find assistance in obtaining a room or a bedroom in a member's house so you can be nearer the hospital. If you remembered to sign up for supplemental insurance, consider using it now. If you couldn't find a way to get help, you might stay in a nearby hotel.

Now is also the time to use those people you have asked to help with the babies while you were pregnant. Because of worries about spreading infection in the NICU, once a baby leaves the NICU, the babies will most likely not be allowed to see one another until all are reunited at home. Unless you and your partner have both been able to swing an extended leave of absence while continuing to keep the cash rolling in, you will be on your own during the day and will need someone to watch the homebound baby while you spend time with the hospitalized ones. If you have had to return to work, your struggle to see both or all babies will be more strenuous. Ask those who offered to help to pick one night per week each (or more if they can) to babysit.

A more detailed discussion of life at home with multiples follows, including more about feeding schedules. Meanwhile, not all of your babies are home yet, and you have to get the food to the hospital and love the ones still there. In reality, you will be fortunate to be able to get to the hospital twice a day. Don't be discouraged if you can make it only once daily. My husband and I took turns with Jack at home, and each went to see Emma once daily to take her milk, try to feed her, and hold her for a time before returning home. The issue is to be sure your hospitalized baby gets attention from you, that you continue to work at bonding with him, and that he continues to receive your breast milk if you are providing it. It may sound unfair, but the baby you have at home has no one but you to care for her, and your hospitalized ones are still being cared for around the clock by skilled and compassionate nurses.

Are You Trying to Scare Me with This CPR Class? Because It's Working!

At some point those nurses will release your fragile, dependent little offspring into your seemingly inept hands. Before any new parent takes her baby home from the hospital, it is the responsibility of the staff to be certain she knows what to do in the event of an emergency. To this end, on the day of or before discharge with your baby, you will be required to attend a class. In this class you are expected to learn how to bathe, diaper, hold, and generally care for your little ones. This includes a video preparing you for the day you have to stick a tube the size of your thumb up the baby's bottom to take his temperature. (In 1975, the date these videos all seem to have been produced based on their hairstyles and disco sound track, they didn't yet know about ear thermometers.)

The part of the class that seems to concern all new parents is the video demonstrating techniques of CPR: what to do if the baby should stop breathing or choke. The difference for a parent of an NICU baby is that she truly believes this scenario will happen the split second after she takes her babies out of their protective cocoon full of omnipresent supervision and gets them into the car. Matters get no better if baby leaves with a home version of "the Machine," called an apnea and bradycardia monitor (see "Apnea/Periodic Breathing" in chapter 15). Nor does it help if the nurses ask whether Mom and Dad would like to take home the baby's ambu bag (a plastic balloon attached to a face mask that is used to provide air pressure and oxygen manually to babies who are unable to breathe). One might think the nurses just assume the baby is going to die the minute they stop caring for it even if they do give reassurance that everything is going to be all right!

This is the moment to take a cleansing breath. The nurses do believe your baby will be okay. So does the neonatologist, or he wouldn't have signed the discharge papers. They want you to feel prepared in the case of a bad event, which is uncommon anyway. What they don't often realize because they do this every day is that their efforts to empower you may actually be loosening the already loose knots of your remaining sanity. You should go ahead and watch the video and consider taking some form of formal CPR class before you deliver. Try to see these as a reminder of your ability to do what needs to be done if it needs to be done. You will have enough to think about once they are all home and you have to begin creating order out of chaos.

Twelve

Bringing the Babies Home

It goes without saying that you should never have more children than you have car windows.

–Erma Bombeck

It all looked so easy, didn't it? The babies were neatly lined up in rows, with the nurses skillfully attending to each and every one of their needs around the clock on a never-changing every-three-hour schedule of feeding, bathing, sleeping, diaper changing, burping, medicating, and holding them. Those nurses smiled, supported, and reassured you, and your babies seemed so content—never unhappy, always just lying there as requested, doing exactly what was needed to allow them to eventually come home with you. You listened to the nurses' instructions, absorbed them fully, and for a short while it seemed as though raising multiples might actually be a doable thing.

Then they came home . . . and reality struck. Freed of the bonds of the NICU, the multiples now seem to take on minds of their own. One wants to sleep while the other wants to play. Two need feeding while the other needs a diaper change. And none of them seems content to lie in bed. Those who aren't crying are throwing up, and they all want to be held! As you slip more deeply into the pit of insanity and despair from which you thought you had emerged weeks before, you begin to believe that you have approached a unique level of hell in which new parents of multiples will, like Prometheus, forever struggle but never achieve their goal, which for them is a single hour of peace and quiet.

You will listen to your friends complain about their single one-year-old and how "difficult" the first few months were for them, and you will decide they have a zero grip on the meaning of the word *difficult.* You might even be tempted to mock their naiveté—if only you had the energy.

You may have other children, but you've never had so many so needy at one time. As you enter into the world of the walking dead, those sleep-deprived souls struggling to eke out an existence among the living, you wonder: How bad would it be, really, to OD on caffeine? At what point does the need to stay awake and cope justify the pain of stapling our eyes open? Does hiring a babysitter just so we can sleep make us negligent and unloving? Is this merely a phase, or is our current pain and suffering indicative of our greater failure as parents and of the future of the world in general? And, above all, how in the world did those ICU nurses control these rascals in the first place?

I want you to realize that advanced skill and hard work are behind the scenes of the calm that surrounded your babies during their stint in the NICU. The nurses have gone through up to four years of college-level learning, and many of them completed extensive education thereafter in both pediatrics and neonatal (NICU) care. Although they love their jobs, your babies are indeed their jobs; the daily routines of a newborn are what they do every day. They are highly trained to provide the care you have seen, and they are often asked to care for acutely ill babies for whom life and death is a breath or two away. As do all medical personnel, the nurses maintain an emotional distance because otherwise they might go mad from all they see and do. It is, therefore, less of a problem for them to insist on routines and schedules and to adhere to them rigorously, and your babies while there responded accordingly. At some point they know, too, that the babies in their care will leave forever.

And what would happen to me, may I ask, if I loved all
the children I said goodbye to?
—Mary Poppins

But now you who have no specialized training, who have seemingly little to offer except that emotional attachment the nurses lacked, who started on this trek with little energy, less reserve capacity, and no objectivity now find yourself at home alone with one or more of your new babies. The NICU team is nowhere in sight, and you must sink or swim on your own as a parent. What can you expect in the first few days and weeks after bringing the babies home, and what, if anything, can you do to improve the chances that your home will be more like the serenity of the NICU and less like center stage at a cockfight?

One of your first tasks is to recognize how your home is and is not like an NICU. Your home is equipped with twenty-four-hour-a-day caregivers like the ICU is; however, you are the caregivers, and there is no night shift to relieve you. Your home has your babies in it, as did the ICU, but it also has your other children, four cats, a dog, and a fish tank, none of which was believed to be hygienic or orderly enough just a few days earlier, or the ICU would have allowed them to come right on inside. Your home, unlike the ICU, also has ringing phones, blaring television sets, and neighbors coming to call to see the new arrivals. Is it any wonder that the babies are not responding the way they did in the NICU? They have noticed that they aren't in Kansas anymore.

How Will I Ever Get Them to Feed/Sleep/Poop Together?

Unless you are a night owl on amphetamines, you may by now fear that you will never survive the process of meeting your babies' needs without winding up in the loony bin from sleep deprivation. You watched the NICU staff follow routines to the letter, but you despair of ever reaching that level of proficiency with time management. You worry that adhering to routines will deprive the children of their emotional needs. Your babies may have come home days or weeks apart from each other, and while one had the continued regimented lifestyle of the NICU, the other has been weaseling his way into your bed at 3 a.m. and begun crying almost at will. You had wanted so much for them to come home but wonder if you will ever again be human. To get the babies on schedule, you must first have—that's right—*a schedule.*

Before you allow your self-esteem to flag because of your sister's or mother-in-law's horror at the idea that you might subject their little kinfolk to regimented lives, remember that unless they had multiples, they have no clue what you are facing. While it might be tenable for one baby to be allowed to behave however she feels the need to behave and to be given as much attention as she wants, it may not be impossible but it is difficult to maintain that type of lifestyle when faced with the prospect of three or four such individuals trying to run the roost. Of all the parents of multiples to whom I've talked, those with the happiest remembrances of the early months were not the ones who recalled babies who slept, ate, pooped, and played, each on their own time frames.

Recognize that, should you choose, you can model your home after the NICU, and your little ones will not suffer. Some experts opine that the presence of regular routines is actually comforting to children because they know what to expect. Find out what the routines of the NICU are and modify them for your home. Wake the children together every three or four hours, change their diapers, feed them, burp them, play with them, change their diapers again (if needed), and let them sleep. Feeding takes thirty to forty-five minutes every three hours for twins and up to one hour for triplets. The rest of the time you spend pumping your breast milk, feeding yourself, and sleeping. Once you've been given clearance by the pediatrician, continue the routine during the day, allowing the kids to sleep as long as they can during the nighttime hours (with certain limitations if you're breast-feeding) so they will learn that nighttime is for sleeping.

Recognize what it was about the NICU that made it such a calm place. Other than the occasional beeping monitors, you would have noticed the nurses speaking softly to one another because they know that loud noises disturb preemies. You would have seen the absence of televisions and ringing phones. Most of all you would have recognized that the full attention of those in the room was focused on the babies present. This absence of distraction you witnessed there is quite helpful in establishing routines that will allow you to retain control of your own sanity. In your home, turn off the TV or allow your other kids to watch it in a room apart from the babies. Turn off the ringer on the phone and allow the answering machine to pick up; you can always return calls when your babies are asleep again. Put a sign on the door asking visitors not to ring the bell or to call ahead and ask to be invited to see you. If something distracts you, it is likely distracting the multiples as well.

Recognize that for the first few weeks at least your attention should be focused on the babies and that while routines are being established the needs of those who can do for themselves will have to wait until after the babies are asleep. Once your multiples have settled in and you are confident in your abilities, you will soon find yourself multitasking again to the nth degree while your babies eat spiders and watch cartoons.

For a pick-me-up, find a quote or quotes you like that will help you get through your day. Repeat one like a mantra as you drag through your eighteenth hour without rest. Those below are some of my favorites, either because they made me smile or because my own parents had drilled them into my head from childhood and Bible lessons:

This, too, shall pass (and, when the hormonal amnesia hits, you may be persuaded to believe you actually enjoyed—or at least didn't mind—this phase of life). —Every Southern mother I ever knew

Any mother [let alone one of multiples, I say] could perform the job of several air-traffic controllers with ease. —Lisa Alther

No one said life was going to be fair. –My mother (and probably every other mother I ever knew)

The most automated appliance in the household is [still] the mother. –Beverly Jones

I can do everything through Christ who gives me strength [yes, I'm a down-home Southern girl at heart]. –Philippians 4:13

Finally, recognize that an emotionally healthy child isn't always a happy child and that your multiples weren't always happy while inside your body even if you couldn't tell. Know that a wet diaper doesn't have to be changed immediately, especially if the baby's skin is healthy and he's fast asleep. Know that if your baby is neurologically intact and his needs have been met—he's dry, he's fed, he's warm—that he may still cry but it's okay to let him cry and teach himself to be calm and return to sleep. One of my favorite books on the subject, *On Becoming Babywise* by Gary Ezzo and Robert Bucknam, M.D., I actually bought and used as my own circadian rhythms approached crisis mode, with night and day dangerously approaching reversal, and found that the approach they advocated using to reestablish routines worked quite well.

Unlike parents who took their babies straight home with them, you have the advantage of bringing home babies used to already established routines. You can simply continue the routines established in the NICU if you have the foresight and emotional fortitude to put your plans into action. If successful, you will find yourself more confident sooner—and might even find time to take a bath sometime during the first two to six weeks before going back to the ob-gyn's office for your checkup. (For information about how to care for yourself after delivery, including care of stitches and so on, please see the next chapter.)

How Am I Ever Going to Get Sleep?

I've mentioned briefly that you need minimal distractions not only for the babies' sense of routine but also because you will need quiet time in which to sleep. Those of you who are mathematically inclined have probably realized by now if you have been blessed with triplets that of the twenty-four hours in a day, you would have only sixteen hours left to eat, bathe, buy diapers, pay bills, and say two words to your equally exhausted spouse before trying to find time to sleep—and that's if the babies behave as scheduled and fail to poop, spit up, cry for no good reason, or activate their A&B monitor (the "apnea and bradycardia" monitor is designed to alert parents if the baby stops breathing or has a low heart rate; see the discussion below or chapter 15, in the section on Apnea/Periodic Breathing, for details). Worse yet, these sixteen hours are available only in two-hour blocks of time. If you need at least eight hours of uninterrupted sleep to thrive each day, you can imagine that within the first two weeks your brain will begin to resemble tapioca pudding.

> I admit it: My husband and I, sometime in the first three months, hired a teenage girl from our church to come to the house for four hours. She watched the twins after their feeding and responded to their cries while we slept. We had never in our lives been so glad to turn over the care of our children to anyone, and we awoke more refreshed, more coherent, and more able to care for them. In retrospect we would have been wise to have done that once or twice a week rather than live the zombie lives we endured during that time. We still ask that young lady to babysit and will be quite unhappy when she leaves us for college soon.

You need sleep to care for your babies! If you have not done so yet, swallow your pride and reach out for assistance. If your parents live nearby, ask them to come over and assist with one or two feedings per day. Even if you breast-feed, they can take care of the diapers and the rest of it while you go back to bed. If you belong to a religious group, ask to have meals made for you in these first few weeks. Hire someone or ask for a favor from a friend, which you will return later, to clean your house and do the laundry. Plan on needing about three months' worth of help from those around you even if it is available only off and on.

I Thought I Had Left All These Wires at the Hospital!

You may notice after bringing the babies home that a miscellaneous item from the NICU may have found its way home with you, having smuggled itself out attached to your baby's body. It is the apnea and bradycardia monitor, otherwise known as the home version of the Machine. It was given to your baby as a parting gift to allow her the ability, though still nonverbal, to scare the living daylights out of you, shattering the sleep you tried to catch while adhering to your schedule. If your baby is sent home with one of these, you may even recall the CPR class and again begin to wonder if your baby wouldn't really be better off back in the ICU where the "real experts" can watch her. The A&B monitor may be accessorized with oxygen tubing for those babies who still have breathing difficulties or with other equipment as needs require, but it is the monitor itself that most of us learn to despise and fear. You may have done everything to eliminate distractions to establish your routines, but the monitor seems to kill the mood every time.

The A&B monitor is designed to alert you when the baby stops breathing, theoretically so you can use that CPR training you received to save her life. They are used until the baby is old enough so that doctors believe the risk she will stop breathing is roughly the same as that of a healthy full-term baby. The monitor usually consists of two rubberized pads held on the baby's chest by a belt that wraps around her body; it is connected to wires running into a piece of electronics roughly the size of a lunch box. The electrodes transmit information about breathing and heart rate to the lunch box, which can then be analyzed by the doctor's office. You will be taught how to read all the flashing gizmos and how to reset the monitor after it has screamed and made you wet yourself.

If you read the Rapid Reference Guide in the back (specifically chapter 15, in the section titled Apnea/Periodic Breathing), you will see that I am not a huge fan of A&B monitors as a general rule, although there may be situations in which they are of benefit (such as a child with a brain injury). As a rule, these monitors have not been proven to prevent SIDS deaths and have been shown to increase the stress level of babies' parents. Nevertheless, the A&B monitor will stay on your baby until the doctor removes it, and I always recommend following your doctor's advice after discussing your concerns with her.

How Will I Ever Feed them All?

Nutritional Requirements for Breast-feeding: As discussed in chapter 4, it is the quality of nutrition you receive as much as the quantity that allows you to become an efficient milk wagon for your hungry brood. Again, I recommend that you talk to a dietician if you need individualized advice, but in general you can expect to consume almost as many calories daily to feed your babies as you did to grow them. An average newborn consumes about three to four ounces of liquid every three to four hours, and if your preemies are like mine, you will be aiming for four ounces every three hours to come out of your swollen breasts.

Considering that one ounce of breast milk contains about 30 calories, at that rate you will need to consume an extra 500 to 900 calories per baby per day to keep your milk supply high enough for the demands placed on you. For a mom of twins, expect to eat 1,000 to 1,800 calories per day extra and still lose the excess weight from the pregnancy. For triplets you need to pack in 1,500 to 2,700 extra calories per day. If you are a mom of quads or more who has successfully breast-fed and even pumped for an extended period of time, consider yourself in the hall of champions. La Leche League should erect a plaque in your honor!

I want to add two special notes here: First, do not use breast-feeding as a weight loss plan. The goal is to provide nutrition to your newborns, not shrink your gut. That will come later! Second, even if you know you will be unable to keep your milk supply at or above the levels demanded for the long haul, still consider pumping or breast-feeding until you can no longer keep up with the demand, or even mixing your milk with formula for as long as possible thereafter. Breast milk has special features that newborns, especially preemies, need to build strong immune systems and to help their internal organs mature. Some studies have suggested that breast-feeding preemies reduces their risk of gastrointestinal diseases common to their early gestational age.

With my twins' bottle dependence and my inability to work and keep my supplies up, I quit pumping when they were around two and a half months old. I was still proud of my ability to create almost ten ounces from each breast per session while it lasted, and looking like a Penthouse pinup for a while didn't hurt my self-esteem any.

Once you have brought all the babies home and have begun to establish routines that will allow you to believe there is life after pregnancy, you will find yourself needing to return to a semblance of life as you knew it. Will you work again? Will you stay home? How will you be able to afford all of this? And when, if ever, will you be a couple again?

Thirteen

Becoming Yourself Again

You've brought the babies home. Reality has struck, and it has hit you squarely and left you with a real set of fears. You allow yourself to ignore for now the gnawing doubt that you will ever be a "good enough" parent. You realize you will have enough time to worry about that later—and that you'll worry about it until you are dead. Right now, at this moment, you have to face the fact that this pregnancy you have fretted about for so long and suffered with so greatly is over and that your life will never be the same. Your task at this moment is to face who (and what) you have become and to learn to be okay with it. It is also your task to finish the administrative details of caring for your babies—and for yourself again.

You've known all along that one singularly important choice needs to be made: Will you try to return to your career? Will you decide to stay at home and raise the kids? How will you maintain both your sanity and the family finances now that the babies have arrived? Are you a bad mommy if you leave your babies? Are you insane if you stay? You may decide instead that what you really need right now is a nice, warm bath.

As you undress in the bathroom, however, you may find that the water you drew for that relaxing bath is running under the door. You have found a more pressing and frightening issue than raising two or more kids at once had initially seemed. You reach your hands down toward your midsection and find alien skin dangling from your breasts to your hips like a deflated balloon. This skin has the oddest sensation when you touch it, as if the dentist just finished numbing your entire abdomen. It feels to your fingers like dough left to rise too long, all warm and full of stretch marks.

As you stand now in ankle-deep water, with those outside trying to break down the door for fear you have drowned yourself, you find yourself completely bewildered. How did you go from bloated to deflated all in one day? Why did the doctor not just go ahead and do a tummy tuck while you were still numb from the epidural? How on earth do they expect you to fold this stuff up and tuck it into your pants?

On the other side of that bathroom door, wondering if you are all right, stands your partner. After waiting all these months and standing by you while you puked, passed out, whined, belched, and kicked him out of the bedroom, he is ready for the green light to "give it a go" again. You realize, of course, that he hasn't yet seen your misshapen body, and you fear—or maybe right now you hope—he will see it and decide he wants nothing to do with you for a little while longer.

At some point your realities will meet. He will see your body, but he will somehow still want sex. You will want intimacy again (you will, I promise) but may fear discomfort. Your body will change for better or for worse, and you do have some control over the way in which it will change. What you learn while you are still pregnant can help you on the road to your life after delivery. What you begin after pregnancy can return you to yourself again.

This chapter will address these issues. I hope to offer suggestions for finding the best balance of career and home for your needs, financing amid chaos, and returning your body (and your psyche) to the place where you can enjoy your partner for what got you pregnant in the first place.

Who Will Care for My Kids if I Return to Work?

Day care for one baby is tough enough to find, you say, so how will I ever take care of so many at once? If you are approaching the end of your pregnancy with trepidation and despair of ever finding a good way to provide care for two or three babies at once, consider yourself among friends. Your sisterhood of working mothers, whether we've had singles or multiples, is full of those who have had to make these same decisions about child care, and we all have ideas about finding the best solution. We have weathered the storms of day care centers, mother's-day-out programs, nannies, au pairs, grandparents, teenage babysitters, and stay-at-home dads. We have suffered the pangs of guilt over our absence from our children and the fear at work that we'll be found to be replaceable should we so much as mention that we have kids. We have found comfort in the medical journals that tell us that the children of working moms are no worse off than those whose moms stayed at home, and anguish about the opinions of those who can't understand why we wouldn't rather just attach them to our breasts permanently.

If you couldn't tell by the way the baby shower went, your friends are waiting anxiously to open their big, fat, opinionated mouths the minute you express an interest in their ideas about raising your children. They will gladly tell you their horror stories in exchange for your feigned interest, and by so indulging them you may find a grain of information of actual benefit to your search. Although it may seem tedious to survey your entire social network, if you plan to return to the workforce, you will need to use every resource at your command—your sisterhood, your patience, your tenacity, and your creativity—to set upon the right path for your babies.

Consider working part-time or alternating your work hours with those of your husband. It may not be the best possible solution since you'll both be tired from work when the babies need you, but it is most likely the least expensive option you might choose. This option also happens to be a pretty potent form of birth control since you will likely not see each other often enough when you have energy enough to enjoy each other.

Another inexpensive solution, should you or your partner be blessed with nonworking parents who are extraordinarily generous with their time, is to ask them to care for the babies during the day. You would go far in preserving the relationship you have with them to offer at least some payment and to express as often as possible how grateful you are for their help. The downside of this option is the implied invitation you may be giving your parents, should they be so inclined, to tell you day in and day out how they expect you to be raising your kids and to try to undo the damage they may think you are doing to their grandchildren during the time they have them. However, if you agree with everything your parents did to raise you, get along well enough with them to negotiate the finer points of child rearing, or are just plain broke and need the help, you will do well to find a way to make this work. In the same vein would be asking members of your extended or religious family for assistance, as many do who have triplets or higher-order multiples, because even if Mom were to stay home, the needs of four or five babies often outpace what she is able to do in the first few months of their lives.

A day care facility is one of the more common options for those unable to stay home or to find family members to help. This is not an inexpensive option and is not generally suitable for babies with health problems that might put them in jeopardy should they be exposed to respiratory illnesses. (In my opinion, any place where small children regularly congregate in enclosed spaces is a fever waiting to happen—such as my twins' first year in preschool.) However, good day care can mean the difference between working and being unable to work, and since the Family and Medical Leave Act went into effect, it has become easier for a woman to leave work for a day or two to care for a sick baby without fearing the loss of her job.

An option many do not adequately consider, perhaps because they think it is too expensive, is a nanny or an au pair. Both are child care providers who keep the children in the children's home. The price for these types of providers can run $250 to $400 per week, depending on your location. While that may be excessive for one child, the price does not change with the number of children. Day care facilities charge per week, per child; in our area the difference between hiring a nanny and schlepping the kids to and from day care is less than $20 per week. If $80 to $100 per month extra sounds like too much, consider the fact that one otherwise healthy child in day care will suffer about eight to ten colds during his first year of life, requiring up to five days off work each time. If you multiply this by the number of babies you are expecting and consider any additional health problems they may be predicted to have, the extra dollars up front may be worth it to you. In the first two years of our twins' lives, I had to leave work three times for less than a day each time because of illness or injury. At the time of this writing they have been in preschool for six months, and my husband and I have been off work for over twenty days, counting the influenza, ear infections, pneumonia, croup, pink eye, and one broken arm (poor baby girl). And preschool expects to be paid whether the kids are there or not.

An au pair is a foreign student who comes to live in your home and is expected to care for the children in exchange for room and board, a salary, and the opportunity to take educational courses and experience America during her down times. The advantage can be that the children have a chance to experience a different language and culture, and be cared for in the comfort, familiarity, and more easily controlled hygiene of their own home. A disadvantage is the limitation—ten hours per day, forty-five hours per week—placed on the au pair's working time, the assumption that she will not work nights, and the usual one-year limit of her visa, after which the search for child care begins again. There are also added costs of hiring an au pair: She must take six semester hours of college-level curriculum, and you will be expected to pony up about $500 to help her in addition to her salary. You will also be responsible for up to $5,000 in the additional expenses involved in applying for her through an agency, interviewing and hiring her, and getting her to the United States.

A nanny (who is different from the occasional or part-time babysitter) may live within or outside the home and provides care for the children as well as doing light cleaning and some laundry and cooking. Although many nannies are lifelong professionals trained in schools much as butlers or maids are, and some even have college degrees in early childhood education, many others (especially outside major coastal metropolitan areas) are older mothers who have raised their own children or are well intentioned and variously talented young people, usually women, who are looking for extra money by caring for your children. The nanny's work hours are limited only by the terms of her contract with you (and I strongly recommend a written contract; see the Resources section for sources). You can more easily control her methods of training the children because she is your employee, she is responsible for only your children (unlike day care), and is less likely to be a member of your family. The disadvantage is that you become, in effect, a small business owner, responsible not only for paying the nanny but for keeping up with her taxes, unemployment, and other government requirements. Many nannies are paid "under the table," but I wouldn't recommend it. There are nanny agencies in some areas that will do the paperwork for you, but the extra fees they charge may or may not be worth it to you.

My favorite resource for information about nannies and au pairs is *The Nanny Book: the Smart Parent's Guide to Hiring, Firing, and Every Sticky Situation in Between* by Susan Carlton and Coco Myers. I also used information I found at *about.com* (search on "Nannies") when formulating the contract we eventually used with "Miss Kim."

Postscript 2003

After I found out I was pregnant with twins, locating child care became an added burden. My sister-in-law, who already had five-year-old and one-year-old girls, had offered to keep our anticipated single baby but could not keep two additional newborns in her house. Day care facilities near our offices either wouldn't take babies under six months old or had room for one baby but not for twins. I started telling every patient, every nurse, and every friend I had my dilemma, hoping to glean ideas from them—Networking 101. To anyone I bored senseless, please accept my deepest apologies!

One day a nurse from our satellite office came to help when we were shorthanded and upon hearing my plight told me of her niece who was unhappy with her current job as a receptionist and was applying for jobs with day care centers. We interviewed her twice, called fifteen of the twenty references she offered us, and hired her just before I gave birth. Thus Miss Kim came into our lives, and the twins loved her from the time they met her, when they were four weeks old, to the day she left us, when they were two and a half years old. I went to work every day with the security of knowing she was caring for them, and knew instinctively when she called that it was indeed an emergency.

Miss Kim still talks to the twins often by phone and comes to visit when she can. She is in the Air Force now, but I have a feeling she will always be a part of Emma's and Jack's lives.

How Can We Survive if I Stay Home?

For many new moms the question of whether to work inside or outside the home is a no-brainer. They have always believed that children should be with their moms and have planned to work part-time or not at all in order to have maximum time with their babies while they are still young. The dilemma for these moms is how they can afford to do it and how they can remain sane should they do it. Again, your tribeswomen can guide you along this path.

One of the toughest questions is how your family will afford three hundred diapers per baby per month, cans of formula, bottles, wipes, car seats, and strollers, and still hope to maintain the standard of living you had when you were both working (or, if you have been at home a while, to add more items to the family budget). The answer is both simple and complex: You find more money or you spend less, or you do both.

First, review the discussion on supplemental insurance, page 25. If you have planned ahead and your babies happen to end up in the ICU for a time, you can use the insurance to build a comfortable nest egg to spend while you take a sabbatical from the working world to care for them. If you are able, you could train for a job from within your home for a few hours each day, using the time when the babies are sleeping. Your husband could take a second job or work extra hours, as happy as that makes any of us. If one or more of your babies have been born with physical handicaps, they may qualify for Social Security Disability Income, which provides monthly payments for their care (see Resources). I don't recommend using credit for spending money, but if you are desperate enough and anticipate only a short-term loss of income that you can recoup, a home equity line of credit or second mortgage can help you afford to stay home for a time before returning to work.

Try to identify areas of your budget in which you allocate nonessential resources—meals out of the house, entertainment, clothes, and the like. Eliminating only one take-out meal each week could save up to $100 per month. We've all been told that in America today it is uncommon for us to have too little money, that more often we have appetites for consumerism that are too big. By limiting unnecessary spending you may find yourself able to care for those babies in the way you believe best without needing additional resources.

Whether you choose to stay home with your babies or continue in the working world, please recognize that as with any job, you will need time off from the job of motherhood, too. New moms need respite from the vomit, poop, pee, and colic of the first months to avoid being sucked into the vortex of brain mush and baby talk. Involve your network again: Ask for one night or day per week that someone else can care for the babies while you care for yourself and your spouse. Utilize a mother's-day-out program; these child care programs, designed to provide a part-time respite for busy moms, are available for three to six hours, two or three days a week at churches, YMCAs, and other places. Find one in the yellow pages or by calling churches and social service organizations near you. Go shopping, even for diapers. Give yourself a manicure. Take a bubble bath. Watch a movie. Remember what it is that makes you who you are, and you will be better able to care for those little ones whom you want to raise to be who they will be.

Finally, here is a brainstorm session for how you can refresh your soul in a short time during these first stressful months. Here are things you can do with even one hour of peace, while the babies nap, from inside your house, for little or no money. You can improve your sense of wellness and recharge your batteries for another day of motherhood with the following:

1. Give yourself a facial
2. Give yourself a manicure or pedicure
3. Take a warm bath, complete with candles and scented water
4. Read an entertaining book
5. Start a scrapbook of your experiences thus far
6. Have a cup of hot tea
7. Close your eyes and appreciate the silence—it's a rare commodity!
8. Practice yoga or do an exercise video or stretches
9. Call your mom or a friend and catch up on gossip or share your frustrations
10. And above all, when you are tired, take a nap; the dishes can wait!

While you consider your options regarding the care and financing of newborns, your partner awaits the return of his beloved. The last thing on your mind, however, somewhere way down on your "to do" list, following "make more milk" and "find two consecutive hours to sleep" is, oh yeah, "have sex with the guy who started all this in the first place." Whatever is going to happen to this completely changed body of yours, and how are you ever going to get comfortable with the stranger in your bed?

Who Is this Stranger in My Bed?

In brief, the stranger lying next to you when you arrive home is hopefully the one who got you pregnant in the first place—and, no, I don't mean the infertility doctor. You have fought together for the health of this pregnancy, and he has been as supportive as he has known how to be. However, he remains in essence the same guy he was before you started this process together. We are taught in medical school that, unlike women, men don't change a whole lot just because they have fathered children, although the later process of parenting can change some of their attitudes about life and their place in it. Your beloved, poor sap, will not understand that you have become a completely different creature from the one whose company he so enjoyed before you had children together.

Your partner may feel like a stranger to you because you can't recall the last time you both lay in bed together or the last time you felt physically comfortable enough to enjoy lying in bed at all. He may feel like a stranger to you because you fear you may have pain if you engage in sex again, so you avoid him to avoid the subject. He may feel like a stranger to you because the two of you are negotiating the rough terrain of multiple parenthood and because the most meaningful conversation you have had in weeks has been about the proper way to reheat frozen breast milk or dispose of the diapers. He may feel like a stranger because the two of you have had separate experiences of the pregnancy and birth of your beautiful children, along with different perspectives of any trouble points along the way. Even if the relationship remained close and loving throughout the pregnancy, you must now deal with changing expectations of your role and the role your partner plays because now you have more than each other to consider.

There may be actual physical reasons for your estrangement. Believe it or not, it is not all in your head or simply situational. It is known that levels of testosterone, the sex hormone responsible for sexual interest and sexual energy, drop in both men and women in the days and months after a pregnancy ends. When the testosterone level drops, so does an interest in sex and sometimes even in the opposite sex altogether. This is why you may find yourself in a home with three new babies, a dog, a cat, and a good friend who was once your lover. The testosterone level begins to rise again in men sooner than in women, sometimes by months to years sooner, causing the man to have a greater interest in sex earlier after parenthood begins than his mate.

If one were to consider this from an evolutionary standpoint in which the goal of sexual activity is the perpetuation of the species, lower testosterone levels would serve to keep attention focused on the care of the newborn until such time as the newborn is able to be more independent. Without the influence of testosterone, the male of the species is more likely to hang around for a while and continue to assist the female in providing for the baby's needs before going off into the woods in search of the next sexual conquest. The female needs a lower sex drive for a longer period of time in order to devote her physical and social energies to the raising of the offspring: breast-feeding, teaching survival skills, and the like. Only after the newborn is capable of moving itself about and feeding itself is it prudent for the female to consider becoming pregnant again.

The bottom line here is this: Ease up on yourself and ask your partner to do the same. You are a different person from the one you were a year ago, and yet you can find a way to renegotiate your relationship and to enjoy each other again. Try to identify those things about your relationship that made you feel close to each other. See how those things are different now from the way they were before you were pregnant. Recognize that on some level you truly are estranged and, just as you did when you met, you need to learn about each other again. Talk it over and get to know each other again. Most of all, make it a priority to spend time together every week even if only for an hour or two. Get babysitters and go to the pizza joint, the mall, the bookstore, wherever you can have what my father calls "unstructured time to relate." A lot of this can be done in the first few weeks while the babies are still in the ICU, perhaps, or while you feel safe that talking won't lead to the next place you're afraid of—sex.

Can I Overcome This Fear of Sex?

You will at some point go to the ob-gyn's office for your six-week-postpartum checkup, and she will examine you to be sure that all your parts have shrunk and moved back into place since your delivery. She will then declare you safe to have intercourse again, and you will beg her not to tell your husband. Meanwhile, his friends at work have been counting the days since the babies were born because he has been extra crabby and they know it is because he hasn't been "getting any" for an eternity. One or two of these friends who have children themselves have probably already informed him of your OB's anticipated declaration because they had anxiously awaited those words themselves at one point in time. You come home possibly to candles or flowers or chocolate because he is desperately trying to tell you he wants some and because it seemed to work on you in the past. At the very least he likely will have bathed and put on his clean underwear as he sits in front of the TV watching *SportsCenter*.

So here you are, facing a hungry partner ready to be satisfied. The pelvic exam at the postpartum checkup wasn't all that fun, and you're not sure you want a repeat performance. At some point, though, you ache to feel normal again, and unless your normal sex drive is the same as a cicada (decades of waiting in the ground for one wild, loud summer night), you'd like to include the pleasures of the flesh as part of that normalcy.

Almost every woman fears sex after childbirth, or it wouldn't be featured so prominently in books, articles, and Web sites. We fear above all that sex will hurt, that perhaps we will have been too stretched to have the same sensations as before, and that our partner may no longer enjoy it as much. The solution to the last two problems is the same, which is to do your Kegel exercises (discussed below).

The answer to the pain during intercourse is lubrication! One of the biggest reasons for painful sex after pregnancy is vaginal dryness. Again, the testosterone levels have fallen, causing tissues to be temporarily somewhat more fragile, and the continued presence of the hormones involved in breast-feeding cause the mucus in the cervix to thicken and become stickier. If you give yourself more time than had been your norm to become aroused and allow the vagina to become well lubricated, you will have an easier time of it. Use artificial lubricant and ask your partner to take it easy the first few times. If you should fail to tolerate completing sex the first time out, be patient with yourself. It will get better.

There are a couple of reasons that we don't feel better after the first few tries. Some women develop a condition after childbirth called vaginismus. This is a contraction of the vaginal muscles in response to a perceived threat of pain. Each episode of intercourse can be painful, leading to more vaginal contractions, more pain, and so on. Another situation in which simple lubrication and gentleness may not help is abnormal healing of vaginal tears or cuts from delivery. Although the doctor should have picked this up at the postpartum checkup, often we don't notice unless you tell us there is a problem. If you should find that your pain gets worse instead of better as you go along, call your doctor and ask her to examine you again. Treatments are available, and you should not have to spend the rest of your life having vaginal pain during intercourse.

Once you no longer have pain, you want to believe you will both continue to enjoy the experience. It is true that the vagina becomes looser after childbirth, and while it shouldn't be an issue for consternation, it often is, for both the man and the woman. A tighter vagina provides more stimulation to both parties. Outside of cosmetic vaginal reconstruction surgery, which as far as I'm concerned is unnecessary, the best and most reliable way to improve sexual enjoyment is the same thing we ask you to do before and after delivery in order to decrease your risk of bladder incontinence. They are called Kegel exercises.

Kegels tighten the muscles of the pelvic wall like arm curls tighten the biceps. Tighter pelvic muscles strengthen your ability to control when you will allow urine to leave your body. They also allow you to control to a certain extent the diameter of your vagina.

To perform a Kegel properly, go to the bathroom and start to pee.

While you are passing urine, stop the stream as best as you can. Right after delivery you may be able to manage nothing better than slowing it to a trickle. Now that you know what muscle movement you should use, begin practicing it everywhere—on the bus, in the car, while reading this paragraph. Try to hold each muscle contraction for as long as you can, and repeat them as often as you can think about it. Within six weeks you should notice a difference in strength and perhaps in enjoyment. Try doing the Kegel during sex and see what your partner thinks of your newfound skill.

Will I Ever Look Attractive Again?

Many of us think right after childbirth that we have just committed the worst possible crime against our physical appearance. We look at our bodies and see the fourteen-inch scar, raw with staples through it. We see the bright red or purple skid marks traversing our squishy bellies. We stare at our legs, newly possessed of purple veins we didn't agree to have, and we wonder: Will we ever be able to wear our clothes, our shoes, our—heaven forbid!—swimsuits again? Are we doomed to look forever like . . . like *moms*?

In a word, yes, we are always going to possess certain marks of our experience. The stretch marks, scar, and veins will fade but will never permanently leave us. The feet will forever be about a half size too big for our old shoes (relax, it's yet another reason to go shopping!). We will, most of us, retain on average about three to five pounds of extra weight, if the gynecology textbooks are to be believed.

We do not, however, need to despair. There are 4 million of us doing this each year in the United States, so we are by no means alone. In addition, the body is an amazingly resilient machine. Within the first year after childbirth most of the mutations of your appearance that you found right after delivery have pretty much corrected themselves, and the few others are well on the way—if you know what to do. In fact, recent evidence—which I want to include because I like what it says—shows that within two years after delivery those of us who had twins will be about the same weight as other women our age, despite having gained more weight during our pregnancies.

You must care for your medical recovery after delivery. If you had a vaginal birth, you will primarily need to avoid intercourse for the first four to six weeks after delivery in order to allow time for the uterus to return to its former size and the cervix to close completely. Failure to wait can result in infection of the uterus and the abdominal cavity (which can cause disability, rehospitalization, or even death) or excessive bleeding from the uterus (which can cause significant problems with anemia). Otherwise, you may bathe, shower, or do pretty much anything else you need to do, although you may be asked not to lift items heavier than about ten pounds in order to reduce your risk of bleeding heavily.

If you had a C-section, in addition to the warnings about sex, you will have an incision to care for. If you had staples or "interrupted" sutures (the railroad track–like stitches we had as kids when we cut ourselves), these will need to come out in about seven to fourteen days (depending on your doctor's preference). If you had so-called subcuticular sutures (those that run underneath the skin in one long connected stitch), they will dissolve on their own. Your doctor's advice may vary from this, but the conservative among us still hesitate to allow you to bathe in a bathtub for the first two weeks for fear of introducing infection when the incision comes into contact with bacteria from the bowels. Showering is universally believed to be okay, and you are encouraged to keep the wound dressed with a bandage for at least the first twenty-four to forty-eight hours. If you are overweight to the point that your stomach overlaps your incision, you may be asked to keep a bandage on longer in order to keep the wound dry. If you wish, you may cover the incision with vitamin E oil once or twice daily, after showers and with dressing changes. This has been shown to reduce scarring, and many cosmetic surgeons recommend it to their patients.

Now for the stretch marks. No matter what your friends or the snake oil salesman on TV tells you, there is no proven way to prevent stretch marks. When the skin stretches, at some point it breaks the bonds of collagen under the skin, and the red tissue underneath shows through. You can inherit stretchy skin from your mom, limiting your stretch marks, or you can limit your weight gain. Unfortunately, if you are having multiples, you will attain roughly the diameter of an oil tanker truck by the time it's all done, and your stretch marks will be your battle scars. Vitamin E oil is widely touted, but by all accounts it has little effect that a good moisturizer can't match for half the price. Within two years the red will have turned to a silvery shade of your flesh tone, and as the belly shrinks, so will some of the stretch marks.

Veins are a similar story. Some things have been shown to decrease your risk of developing varicose veins, such as avoiding crossing your legs for long periods of time, elevating your legs as often as possible, and wearing support hose (to the waist, not knee highs because of an increased risk of blood clots). Minimizing excess weight gain reduces the pressure inside the veins, and regular exercise keeps excess blood from pooling inside and stretching them. These, too, will look their best by two years after delivery.

Finally, the belly and the weight thing. As you will remember, in order to have a healthy multiple pregnancy you needed to gain between thirty-five and fifty pounds, most of which you devoted to the development of the babies. A substantial minority portion of the weight gain you accumulated was designed to build your blood volume, provide for adequate fluid around the babies, and develop and enlarge your breasts for making milk. A few pounds of that weight gain were, yes, fat, designed to provide cushion in critical areas and storage of reserve calories in case of a food shortage. In the first six weeks you will have lost over half the weight just from the delivery of the babies, and several more pounds as you got rid of the extra fluid inside your blood vessels and legs. This happens because after your body senses that the pregnancy is over, it releases the excess fluid from the blood vessels and soft tissues (remember the tree trunks your legs had been?) into the kidneys, where it is removed from your body as urine (yes, that's why you lived in the bathroom in the first few days after delivery).

Once the fluid and the babies are gone, the rest is up to you. Most likely the weight gained that is not lost within the first two years after delivery will stay forever. Once you have been cleared by your OB, you must begin to exercise and watch what you eat if you hope to regain your appearance. Weight loss, regardless of the reason for weight gain, is always a matter of calories in, calories out. You should always be cautious not to short yourself so many calories that you compromise your milk supply, but habits begun now can reap great benefits for the future.

Eat only enough calories to maintain your basic needs and your calorie requirements for breast-feeding (see chapter 12). If you need help, ask your doctor to send you back to the dietician for a consultation. Focus on eating healthy calories, those most likely to be used for milk and a healthy metabolism and less likely to be stored as fat. These include fruits and vegetables, lean meats, and complex carbohydrates (not simple sugars, which are rapidly released into the bloodstream and more likely to be stored).

Focus, too, on drinking at least as many ounces of water and other noncaffeinated beverages as you produce in breast milk each day, then add another two or three eight-ounce glasses to account for perspiration. When you begin to exercise, add an additional eight-ounce glass for each fifteen to thirty minutes that you spend exercising. This will help ensure that you do not become dehydrated and lose your milk supply, which you will do before your body allows your health to suffer from dehydration.

Remember that you have not been using your body in the same way you once did, so start exercising more slowly—but by all means start exercising. Begin with gentle stretches and exercises to strengthen your core muscles of the back and abdomen, such as yoga or Pilates. Many of us have back pain and bad postures from lying in bed for half of our pregnancies, and without a strong core and good posture it is difficult to find the energy to move further. After the first few weeks add walking, biking, or swimming, whatever will increase your heart rate and make you sweat. Practice exercising at least five days a week even if it requires that you walk the stairs in your house while the babies sleep, push them in the stroller around your neighborhood, or do an exercise video. Make it your goal to do thirty minutes daily and watch the weight come off. In fact, the minimum daily activity level for a healthy lifestyle is thirty minutes on most days of the week.

Sound unrealistic? To date I have counseled thousands of patients about diet and exercise, and have found no one yet who could not do at least the minimum. For the most part I have found that we all (myself included) come up with excuses rather than reasons, and it all comes down to priorities.

If you believe you are too tired to exercise, know that after twenty minutes of aerobic exercise, hormones called endorphins are released by the brain. These hormones make us feel more relaxed and energetic than we had before we exercised, help us sleep more soundly (when we aren't being awakened by the multiples), and renew our sense of well-being. If you can just make yourself do it, you will feel better afterward, no matter how much sleep you lost the night before with the triplets.

If you believe you are too busy to exercise, understand that you have time to do everything to which you give high priority, and in my mind your long-term health (not just your physical appearance but your mental health and how you will feel when you are elderly) are of such high importance that they should come second only to the care you give your infants. If you work, do your exercise during lunch, as I do (because I, too, have a chaotic home life full of twins and their stuff). If you have chosen the more-than-full-time job of motherhood of multiples, exercise during one of the scheduled nap times for the babies that you have incorporated into the NICU-like household you created. If that can't be done, use your imagination to find time. Form a partnership with other mothers in your neighborhood or find a similarly motivated partner in your Mothers of Multiples group. Use the time your friends have promised to babysit for you to get the job done. I firmly believe in the value of exercise and do everything I can as often as I can not only to preach the word but to serve as a good example.

Postscript 2003

After six weeks at bed rest, nineteen hours of labor, two vaginal deliveries, and two months of pumping, feeding, diapering, and sleeping, I returned to work and my back hurt. *I tried exercising but found myself unable to walk even a block without becoming short of breath. I became unable to lift a five-pound baby without pain and had trouble sleeping even when the babies weren't fussing.*

Believing I should practice what I preach when dealing with chronic pain, I went for the first time ever to a fitness center. I chose the one at Mercy Hospital because of its proximity and its atmosphere: two blocks from my office (can't argue a lack of availability because I can do this at lunch), full of cardiac patients (can't use the excuse that I hate the "meat market" ambience). And at less than $30 a month, I couldn't argue it was too expensive.

I met Angela, my trainer, during the introductory visit. She asked me my goals. I said I'd really like to be able to lift my twins without my back hurting, and she said, "No problem. Take about six weeks. What else?" Told her I wished to look like I hadn't had kids, and she said, "It'll take some work, about six months, but we can do it. Do you have a pipe dream?"

Now I've always been a rather bookish sort, never good at the fitness thing, and couldn't even walk for exercise at this point, but I really admired what it took to be an endurance athlete. From some corner that harbors irrational thought in the recesses of my mind, I let it slip: "I've always thought it would be cool to do a triathlon." Instead of laughing at the blobby ex-pregnant lady, Angela said simply, "Give it a year, and we'll get it done."

For eight months I faithfully performed the steps she had outlined on my five-by-seven cards, doing weights a couple of days a week and cardio three to four days. She increased my intensity as she saw me improve, and then I saw it: an ad for the inaugural Lighthouse Triathlon. Five-hundred-yard swim, thirteen-mile bike, and a 5K run. I asked Angela to draw up a training schedule for me, and in August 2002 I completed it! One hour and forty-five minutes, but no injuries.

And I was buff! *I found myself in the best shape of my life, skinnier than I had been in high school and with more energy than I had thought possible.*

I resolved to renew my efforts at encouraging my patients to adopt healthy lifestyles and refusing to hear their excuses as to why time was unavailable.

And I decided to write a book to try to help other women survive multiple pregnancy.

PART 4

Rapid Reference Guides

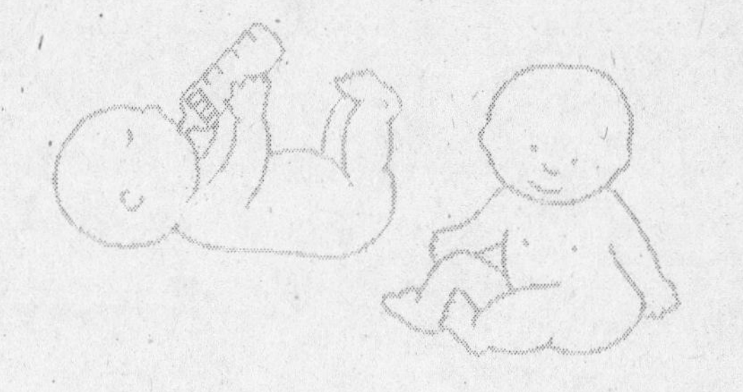

Fourteen

Rapid Reference Guide to Pregnancy Complications

This section and the one that follows are designed to provide outlines of problems you may encounter in a multiple pregnancy. I will give for each problem the causes and risk factors, if known, the possible symptoms you might have, what could happen if the problem is not addressed, when to call the doctor, and what he or she will likely do about the problem.

If you are already prone to anxiety attacks by the very thought of having multiples, *skip this section* and go directly to chapter 16. If you should encounter a problem down the road, you will likely find it here.

Please note: This is intended only as a general guide to some of the more common problems you may face. It is not intended to falsely reassure you or to overly concern you. Although I list some of the common treatments for each problem, please be aware that medicine changes rapidly, and what may have been good practice at the time this book was written may be out of date tomorrow. Also, the standards of practice vary from community to community and must be individualized from patient to patient, so if your doctor does not do exactly what is listed, feel free to ask her about it, but do not assume that she is not following the best practice for your pregnancy.

Preterm Labor

Definition. Preterm contractions happen all the time. It is important to note that preterm labor is simply preterm contractions that dilate and efface (thin) the cervix. Other contractions (those that do not result in the cervix changing) may or may not be a cause for concern, but only after you have been evaluated can the doctor know for certain.

Causes and risk factors. There are many causes for preterm labor and some reasons that are as yet unknown. Any situation in which the uterus can take no more stress—too much volume inside it, too little nutrition or blood flow nourishing it, or too much illness, stress, or injury to the mother—can cause it to try to expel its contents (your little ones) too early. You might consider it nature's way of preserving the adult female for another attempt at pregnancy in order to preserve the species at the expense of the young and helpless.

Risk factors for preterm labor include but are not limited to the following:

1. Multiple gestation—tops the list every time (lucky us!)
2. Previous history of preterm labor and delivery
3. Having abdominal surgery during pregnancy
4. Abnormalities of the uterus (DES exposure, cone biopsy, cervical surgery)
5. Previous abortions
6. Illness that causes high fever—any type will suffice, but kidney infections are a separate risk factor in and of themselves
7. Bleeding or irritability of the uterus in or after the second trimester
8. Smoking

Preterm labor is associated with, but has not been shown conclusively to be due to, age above thirty-four or less than eighteen, stress, and jobs that require heavy lifting.

Symptoms. The classic symptom of preterm labor is the presence of regular contractions that can be painful. Not all women have the classic symptom, however, so you should watch out for any increase in vaginal discharge, lower back pain, pelvic pressure, diarrhea, extreme fatigue, or bleeding. You might also have fever that may or may not be related to an infection.

What could happen next. If left untreated, your babies could be born. As miserable as you might feel now, you don't want preterm babies if you can help it. The problems often faced in the NICU (see next chapter) are almost always associated with babies born too early and/or too small.

When to call the doctor. Doctors sometimes differ in their recommendations, so by all means follow your physician's instructions. I tell my patients to call if they feel contractions that are regular and every ten minutes for one hour, if they feel leaking or have bleeding, or if they have other concerns that something is just "not quite right."

What the doctor may do about it. Depending on how far along you are in your pregnancy, your doctor may or may not choose to try to stop your labor. She will certainly try to identify and treat any illnesses or abnormalities of the pregnancy that could have caused the labor in the first place, although in the absence of other findings she may very well simply chalk it up to the fact that humans aren't supposed to deliver two or three years' worth of reproductive potential at once.

If it is determined that labor must be stopped, she will give you a variety of medications to try to stop your contractions. Some of the most commonly used medications are listed below, along with the most common (and much less likely but potentially serious) side effects you might experience. I do this not to frighten you (I certainly would rather you call your doctor and get treatment if necessary than ignore your symptoms and deliver premature babies) but because I firmly believe in true informed consent. You should know that what we recommend is designed to be helpful but that there might be side effects. There is regional variation in your doctor's preference, but the options include these:

1. Terbutaline (Brethine), an asthma medicine related to albuterol (the rescue inhaler that asthmatics use) that can cause your heart to race and your body to have profound fatigue.

Much less often it can cause a buildup of fluid in the lungs known as pulmonary edema, so if you have shortness of breath with this medicine, you must call your doctor.

2. Magnesium, a mineral given by IV that can cause weakness of all muscle groups (since the uterus is, in fact, a muscle unit), including, if given in too large of a dose, suppression of the ability to control breathing. You should be in the hospital if you are receiving this medication, and nurses should be checking your reflexes every one to two hours. You will also have blood drawn every few hours to check the magnesium level in your body.
3. Nifedipine, a blood pressure medication that can cause a slow heart rate, low blood pressure, dizziness, and headache. It only rarely causes serious problems, but should you have a sensation that you might pass out or have shortness of breath, call your doctor immediately.

Your physician will also assess the risk of your imminent delivery, should it happen, and will do her best to minimize the risks of the babies being born too early. Steroids given at least twenty-four hours before delivery is expected can decrease your babies' risk of breathing trouble after birth. This has been shown to be of great benefit if you are between twenty-seven and thirty-two weeks, although since you are expecting multiples, I should tell you that it remains unclear whether steroids help in multiple pregnancy.

Hypertension and Preeclampsia/Eclampsia

Definition. Hypertension is a blood pressure reading above 140/90 or a change from normal of more than 30 points on the top number or 15 points on the bottom number during pregnancy.

Preeclampsia is the presence of hypertension plus a finding of protein in the urine or edema after twenty weeks of pregnancy. Eclampsia is defined as seizures in a woman with preeclampsia in whom no other cause for seizures is known.

Causes and risk factors. The direct cause is complex and is still under study, but it has to do partly with the interaction between the baby's placenta hormones and the mother's hormone system of the kidneys and the lining cells of her blood vessels. We do know that only delivery of the placenta or placentas will cure the condition.

It is not an adequate analogy, but it is convenient to say that the symptoms and complications associated with preeclampsia and eclampsia are due to swelling of the tissues in the body: Brain swelling causes severe headaches and vision trouble, and may later cause seizures; liver swelling causes abdominal pain and may cause the liver to malfunction; kidney swelling causes kidneys to leak protein and to poorly control fluid balance, resulting in arm, face, and leg edema.

Risk factors are complicated, too, but include these:

1. First-time pregnancy, because Mom is not acclimated to all the immune factors of Dad's body, and now half of Dad is inside Mom's body in the form of a baby and placenta
2. A pregnancy with a new dad, for the same reasons
3. Maternal age greater than thirty-four
4. A past history of high blood pressure in Mom
5. Multiple pregnancy
6. Diabetes and lupus, because they cause changes to blood vessels
7. Kidney diseases in Mom

Symptoms. Most women first have what are called signs rather than symptoms. This means that the doctor often notices the condition before the patient actually feels discomfort as a result of it. The signs of preeclampsia are those that define the illness, namely, high blood pressure, protein in the urine, and/or edema, particularly of the face and hands. However, knowledge of the symptoms is useful; they include these:

1. Headache, usually severe and different from a woman's chronic headaches—which is important not because women with

headaches are more likely to get preeclampsia but because the headache of preeclampsia is caused by increased pressure inside the brain and usually feels different from a usual headache—and is not improved with her usual medication or rest

2. Blurred vision, spots, or abnormal visual patterns, or blindness in one or both eyes (also due to increased pressure inside the brain)
3. Pain in the middle or right upper part of the abdomen that is not related to babies' movements (due to the aforementioned swelling inside the liver against its relatively nonelastic covering)

What could happen next. Preeclampsia is a serious medical condition of pregnancy; eclampsia is an emergency. If allowed to progress, these conditions could lead to the mother becoming blind, brain damaged, or deaf, to severe blood loss, to liver and kidney failure, and possibly to the death of the mother and/or the babies.

When to call the doctor. Again, every doctor has his or her own spiel about when to call. My personal preference is that if a woman has severe headache, blurred or funny vision, pain in the belly not related to the baby moving, or swelling of the face or hands, she should call immediately. The most important side note here is that you must be careful to always keep your regularly scheduled follow-up appointments with your doctor because early detection and intervention is more effective than trying to treat something that has already happened.

What the doctor may do about it. Your physician's response depends on the severity of your disease as he sees it moment by moment. Mild cases often require nothing more than reduced activity and maybe less salt in the diet, and more frequent doctor's office visits for monitoring your condition and the health of the babies. The most severe cases require hospitalization and administration of medications to reduce the risk of seizure and to assess your need for ending the pregnancy versus the babies' health risks if they were to be delivered at that time.

Preterm Premature Rupture of Membranes (PPROM)

Definition. The babies and the fluid that surrounds them are protected from the outside world by a sac of membranes. This sac will rupture at some point during labor. Premature rupture of membranes is the loss of integrity in this sac before labor has started. Preterm rupture of membranes, whether premature or accompanied by labor, is what may occur before thirty-seven weeks of pregnancy.

Causes and risk factors. The causes are unknown, but women who experience PPROM are also the women who have the most risk factors for preterm labor.

Symptoms. The primary symptom of PPROM is the presence of fluid leaking from the vagina, although contractions of the uterus may or may not be present at the same time.

What could happen next. Once the membranes have ruptured, the unborn child is exposed to the outside environment. Babies whose mothers have PPROM for too long can develop infections, and if delivery must happen, they face the potential complications of premature birth. Babies need their amniotic fluid not only for protection against infection but also for expanding their developing lungs and for buoyancy within which their skeletons can develop. If the membranes rupture before twenty-five weeks of pregnancy, babies can be born with permanently underdeveloped lungs or with deformities of the skeleton.

When to call the doctor. I caution my patients to call if they feel a leakage of any fluid that may be from their vagina. If it turns out to be urine or semen instead (which it often does on exam), I'm happy to be able to tell Mom to go home.

What the doctor may do about it. You will likely be hospitalized for the duration. Depending on how far along you are in the pregnancy, your physician may do nothing more than monitor you for signs of infection and let you deliver the babies. If it is determined that your babies need more time, you will be monitored daily for signs of infection or of distress in your babies. Those steroids mentioned before—to help the babies' lungs mature if preterm delivery is predicted—are controversial here, especially if an infection of the uterus is suspected; therefore, your doctor will carefully explain to you the risks versus the benefits of this approach.

Vaginal Bleeding

Definition. Any spotting or flow of blood from the vagina.

Causes and risk factors. Vaginal bleeding has several causes depending on the trimester in which it occurs. In the first trimester, it may have to do with the transfer of responsibility for maintaining the pregnancy from the ovaries to the developing placenta, although it may also be a sign of miscarriage. In the second trimester, placenta previa and placental abruption are potentially serious causes (see below). In the third trimester, both placenta previa and abruption can cause bleeding, but so can the bloody show of labor, which is a normal event. Manipulation of the cervix, such as through intercourse or procedures, or cervical infection can also cause bleeding.

Here are two of the most serious causes of bleeding:

1. Placenta previa, a condition in which the placenta implanted itself in the part of the uterus that overlays or contains the cervix
2. Placental abruption, a situation in which the placenta peels away from its attachment to the uterus

Symptoms. With placenta previa there are frequently no symptoms other than bleeding, which varies from spotting to hemorrhage. The blood loss may occur for no reason but may follow intercourse or a physical examination of the cervix. It may also occur after labor contractions have started.

Placental abruption usually presents with bleeding, although the blood loss may be disguised for a time if it is contained within the uterus.

Other findings include the presence of a tender uterus with or without contractions, lower back pain, and fetal distress or shock.

What could happen next. Severe blood loss in Mom and babies may result if a woman with an unrecognized placenta previa is allowed to deliver vaginally. The same goes for untreated placental abruption, although it is not the route of delivery that is at issue here but, rather, the risk of continued bleeding inside the uterus leading to anemia, fetal distress, and shock or death for all involved.

When to call the doctor. You should call immediately if you experience bleeding during your pregnancy. Your doctor will provide you with specific guidelines, but never hesitate to call if you have concerns.

What the doctor may do about it. When you call with bleeding, especially in the late second or third trimester, your doctor will want to identify the cause. She may choose to do an ultrasound first before inserting an examining finger, to be certain of the location of the placenta if she doesn't already know. She would be doing this to rule out a placenta previa before she takes the chance of making it worse. She may also do blood tests and/or tests on the vaginal fluid to help her make a diagnosis.

For both conditions, treatment is a matter of balancing the life of the baby against that of the mother. Placenta previa can often be controlled with bed rest, either in or outside the hospital, monitoring of the blood count, and avoidance of all vaginal manipulation, including sexual intercourse. Your doctor will have blood available for a transfusion if she is concerned about sudden blood loss, and she will monitor your babies for signs of health and growth by ultrasound. She will work as hard as possible to keep the babies inside you until they have the best chance of healthy life outside you even if it means repeated blood transfusions. You will most likely have a C-section for delivery unless the placenta "grows" out of the way, as they sometimes do.

Your doctor will monitor you in a similar fashion for abruption, but she has a tricky job in managing your risks against those of your babies. She will try to buy you as much time as possible, but you will likely remain in the hospital until you have delivered. She may try to stop the contractions as she would for preterm labor, and she will support your blood volume with fluids and your oxygen levels as needed. Once the risks to your health outweigh the benefit to your children of additional time inside your body, she will proceed to deliver you. Vaginal versus C-section birth is somewhat controversial here and depends on the experience and confidence of your doctor given your particular case.

Twin to Twin Transfusion Syndrome (TTTS)

Definition. TTTS happens only in pregnancies where there is only one placenta for both babies ("monochorionic" multiples). These babies share some blood vessels within the placenta, and one baby's circulatory system may "steal" blood from the system of the other baby through these vessels. TTTS is present in 5 to 15 percent of monochorionic twins and may be a part of the "vanishing twin syndrome" in which a pregnancy appears to contain twins early on but the "twin" vanishes during development. There is a rare form of this disorder, present in about one in a hundred of these twins, called twin reversed arterial perfusion syndrome, in which one twin has no heart but the circulation of the other supports them both.

Causes and risk factors. The cause is, as stated above, that one baby steals blood from the other as a result of their shared circulatory system within the placenta. The only risk factor is that the babies share a placenta.

Symptoms. Mom generally has no symptoms. The twins will show problems during their ultrasound exams. One will be growing much faster than the other, and the smaller twin may have a decreasing amount of amniotic fluid supporting its growth, while the larger one may show signs of heart failure.

What could happen next. If left untreated, TTTS has a 90 to 100 percent mortality rate for both twins. If one dies before the other, the surviving twin may be left with permanent heart, brain, or other problems. With treatment, survival can climb to 60 to 80 percent.

When to call the doctor. This is not so much a when-to-call issue as it is another example of the importance of keeping regular follow-up appointments with your doctor.

What the doctor may do about it. There are several approaches to treating TTTS. Medications can be given to Mom to support the babies' hearts and decrease kidney output. The primary medications are digoxin and indomethacin, an anti-inflammatory. The nutritional supplement Boost is being studied for prevention of TTTS and appears promising.

Amniocentesis, performed as often as necessary, is the most commonly used procedure. The needle is inserted into the sac of the too-large twin to draw off the excess fluid and allow the smaller twin more of a chance to grow. The disadvantage is that the underlying process isn't treated, so some problems, such as brain damage, can still happen.

An old technique for treatment is the early delivery or selective abortion of the smaller twin. This usually results in certain death for one of the babies for the benefit of the other. This requires the discussion of the moral and ethical dilemmas surrounding life and death that I won't cover here. It is not frequently performed, however, because the risks of such a procedure are often greater than the risks of continued amniocentesis.

A new technique being practiced at some high-risk facilities is laser surgery of the placenta to eliminate the abnormal blood vessels. As of this writing, it is not yet the standard of care; although the survival rate appears to be similar to amniocentesis and the risk of brain damage appears to be less, studies are still ongoing. If you face this illness for your children, I recommend that you ask about the nearest center of study for the laser approach and whether you would be a candidate for joining the study.

Conjoined Twins

Definition. Conjoined twins are identical twins formed from the same egg that incompletely split around the thirteenth to fifteenth day after conception. They can be joined at any portion of their bodies, and the type of connection is named based on the most prominent feature where they are attached, be it head, abdomen, back, and so forth. Conjoined twins are extremely rare—rarer than several conditions not included in the book—but are included because of the continuing interest in their existence.

Causes and risk factors. As mentioned above, conjoining happens when the egg doesn't completely split. No particular risk factors are identified for this rare condition.

Symptoms. None. The condition is usually discovered by ultrasound.

What could happen next. The twins can have a higher risk of the conditions common to twins during pregnancy. If undiscovered, Mom and babies can die during an attempted vaginal delivery. After birth they may have a high risk of complications if separation is attempted.

When to call the doctor. Anytime you want to talk about it. The need for good communication with your doctor is of the utmost importance when there are possibly difficult decisions to be made.

What the doctor may do about it. Depending on your moral and religious beliefs, you may be asked if you want to end the pregnancy. If you should not desire that, you will be carefully monitored and the babies' connections to each other carefully assessed to evaluate the possibility of separating them safely. A C-section delivery is preferred to reduce the risk of injury to the babies.

Fetal Loss

Definition. Fetal loss is as it sounds: One or more babies dies while still in the womb. The "vanishing twin syndrome," in which two or more babies are seen on an initial ultrasound but one disappears later, is the earliest form of this. In fact, only about 50 percent of twin pregnancies seen in early ultrasound actually result in the delivery of two live children. This would mean that up to one in fifteen pregnancies actually started with twins! Overall, the risk of one twin dying is 2 to 5 percent, with a higher risk for twins who share a placenta, and the risk in a triplet or higher pregnancy is 14 to 17 percent.

Causes and risk factors. The exact causes are unknown, and there are many reasons for one of a set of multiples to die. Risk factors include the presence of one placenta, raising the question of TTTS (see above) or of fetal abnormalities (birth defects) as a cause.

Symptoms. Sometimes you might experience vaginal bleeding after the death of one baby, but frequently you won't know it until the follow-up ultrasound.

What could happen next. As sad as it can be to lose a baby, even one still in the womb, the risks to Mom and the surviving baby/babies require attention. After one twin dies, the other has a 20 percent or more chance of death and up to a 5 percent chance of being mentally handicapped or of having cerebral palsy. Again, those babies who had shared a placenta with the deceased twin have the higher risk, raising the possibility that toxins released by the dead twin invaded the body of the other or that blood clots due to the demise clogged the placenta of the surviving twin. What happens to the dead twin depends in large part on how far along the pregnancy is at the time as well as whether or not the twins shared a placenta or amniotic sac. In the first trimester, most are reabsorbed into the "products of conception," becoming a collection of inactive tissue in or around the placenta or lining of the uterus. Some are believed to be absorbed by the surviving twin, and although this is a fallacy, many people believe that certain tumors, particularly those containing hair and teeth, were their long-lost twin. Later in pregnancy the dead fetus remains relatively intact but decomposes, causing the release of the toxins discussed. The dead twin will typically remain in the uterus until the other is delivered.

One of the big risks to the survivor is prematurity. Fifty to 80 percent of twins who had lost a twin delivered before they were full term.

Mom has risks, too. Due to the toxins released by the dead fetus,

Mom can sometimes find her blood-clotting system attacked, leading to the possibility that she might bleed to death herself. This is not common but is important to mention because she will need to be monitored. A more common condition is the grieving process many women experience even in early pregnancy with the loss of a child. As with any miscarriage, the loss can lead to depression.

When to call the doctor. Anytime you have concern. If you have been told that one of your multiples is deceased, watch for symptoms such as easy bruising or bleeding, abdominal pain, vaginal bleeding, or contractions. Also be aware that you are at risk for depression. Call the doctor if you experience uncontrollable feelings of sadness that overwhelm your ability to cope, especially if they are accompanied by a sense of hopelessness or helplessness.

What the doctor may do about it. The doctor will want to monitor your pregnancy and your health after the death of one baby. She will check periodically for signs of bleeding disorders in your blood tests and will monitor the health of the surviving baby/babies to determine the best time for delivery to limit the risk of brain damage while preserving viability.

Another task your physician has is to monitor you for signs of abnormal grief or depression. Treatment is quite safe and effective, but failure to treat severe depression can result in further complications for your pregnancy and for after delivery. It is important to feel accepted and that you are welcome to ask questions of your physician. It is also important to recognize when you need assistance with your emotional health.

Fifteen

Rapid Reference Guide to Complications in the NICU

This section is a general overview of some of the problems you might face with your babies when they are born.

Please note: This is intended only as a general guide to some of the more common problems you may face. It is not intended to falsely reassure you or to overly concern you. Although I list some of the common treatments for each problem, please be aware that medicine changes rapidly, and what may have been good practice at the time this book was written may be out of date tomorrow. Also, the standards of practice vary from community to community and must be individualized from patient to patient, so if your doctor does not do exactly what is listed, feel free to ask her about it, but do not assume that she is not following the best practice for your newborns.

I will only be dealing with some of the most common issues and only with those common issues that frequently present themselves in the NICU. Chronic diseases would take too much of your valuable time to discuss and might provide you with even more to worry about, should you be so inclined.

Although I have listed a few of the risks for some of the treatments outlined, please be aware that every procedure in medicine carries with it some risks, and know that you have the right to informed consent, meaning that you have the right to ask the doctor what might happen to your babies because of the treatment and what might happen if they don't receive treatment. You also have the right to take that information and make the best decision you can make about whether to agree to that treatment for your child. Often, when emergencies arise, we have little time to talk before we act in what we believe to be your child's best interest, but even then that does not mean you should not ask questions if you have concern.

Respiratory Distress

Definition. There are several types of respiratory trouble. Two are most common in preemies, and to the untrained eye they can look like distress.

1. Transient tachypnea of the newborn: Present in near-term, full-term, or large preterm babies, this is a condition with little cause for concern. It lasts about three days and resolves on its own. The baby will breathe rapidly but will not develop distress.
2. Hyaline membrane disease (HMD): The true respiratory distress of the newborn, this is primarily a disease of preterm infants, although any baby can have it. It consists of rapid breathing (more than sixty times per minute) with signs of distress (blue skin color, use of neck muscles for breathing, or sucking in of the chest wall with each breath) that lasts more than forty-eight hours or gets worse. Doctors will do a chest X-ray to confirm the diagnosis and to follow the course of the illness.

Causes and risk factors. HMD results when the baby is unable to make enough of a substance called *surfactant*. Surfactant coats the lung linings and helps the lungs open with each breath. Without enough surfactant, babies (especially preterm and weak or small ones) are unable to muster enough strength to open the lungs fully and get good breath. In the presence of enough surfactant, some babies can still get HMD due to heart problems or other troubles, but they are less common.

Risk factors that increase a newborn's odds of HMD are these:

1. Prematurity.
2. Male sex
3. Family history of breathing problems, especially in infancy
4. Uterine infection that involves the babies
5. Having been born by C-section, because the pressure generated when the baby passes through the birth canal helps to push fluid out of the baby's lungs, and those born by C-section haven't had that benefit
6. A labor troubled by the baby's loss of oxygen at some point before birth, known as asphyxia
7. Hydrops fetalis, a condition in which the baby's tissues, including the lungs, collect too much fluid due to Rh factors (Mom versus baby blood type problems) or other illnesses

Symptoms and signs. Babies with HMD have breathing trouble at birth that becomes more severe as time goes on. They have cyanosis (blue skin color) and become dependent on more and more oxygen to keep their skin pink. With each breath, the babies' nostrils flare, and they may make a grunting noise when they let out their breath.

What could happen next. If the distress is not treated, babies can die rapidly. Their lungs may fill with more fluid, and they eventually lose the strength to work as hard as they need to in order to survive. Some babies do survive but can be left with a chronic lung disease similar to asthma and emphysema called bronchopulmonary dysplasia (BPD). BPD is too big a topic to cover here and isn't often presented in the NICU.

Fortunately, we have treatment for HMD, and with appropriate treatment babies have a better than 90 percent chance of survival, depending on their level of prematurity and any other problems they may face.

What the doctor will do about it. Your neonatologist will monitor your babies very closely, looking for the earliest possible signs that they might need help with their breathing. Oxygen is usually provided, and breathing will be assisted to the level of need of the child. The most common scenario is for your baby to be put on a ventilator until the condition resolves. A tube will be inserted into the baby's airway (called intubation) and the tube connected to a machine that provides pressurized airflow at preset intervals to support the baby's work of breathing (see chapter 11). Sometimes, however, air can be forced into your baby's lungs by the use of a positive pressure machine attached to a mask on the baby's face.

New and great things are evolving in this area of newborn care. One miracle drug that is in widespread use is surfactant replacement. It is given to reduce the severity of breathing trouble by providing the very thing that has been lacking in babies with HMD. Studies have shown no long-term downside to giving surfactant, but what they have not shown is change in the development of long-term problems related to prematurity.

One particular problem to ask the neonatologist about is your children's risk of something called retinopathy of prematurity (ROP). ROP is a disease of the still-developing eye caused by overgrowth of blood vessels in the retina (at the back of the eye). It is found most often in premature babies, especially those who needed oxygen treatment. If left undiagnosed and untreated, it can cause vision problems, including blindness. However, if your babies need oxygen to live, you may simply need to know about this problem so you can advocate for appropriate follow-up care later. Each baby that has been on oxygen during his or her stay in the NICU will require an office visit with a pediatric ophthalmologist (a doctor who went through the four years of medical school followed by a residency in medical and surgical diseases of the eye) within the first two weeks to one month after hospitalization. You might advocate for the ophthalmologist to see the babies in the NICU if it is expected they will be there for more than a few weeks.

Apnea/Periodic Breathing

Definition. Apnea is when the baby stops breathing for more than twenty seconds. This may happen with or without something called bradycardia, in which the heart rate decreases. Periodic breathing is when baby stops breathing frequently for short periods of time during a twenty-second period. Both of these conditions are common. Apnea happens in 50 to 60 percent of premature babies, and periodic breathing happens in another 30 percent or so.

Causes and risk factors. Theories abound, although an exact cause is still unknown. It may have to do with immaturity of the brain in controlling the breathing process, with overactivity of a normal reflex designed to protect the baby's airway, or with sleep pattern problems or muscle weakness.

Risk factors for apnea and periodic breathing include:

1. Prematurity
2. Having a sibling who died of SIDS
3. Neurological disease
4. Hypothermia
5. Low blood sugar
6. Infection, including sepsis and necrotizing enterocolitis (see below)

Symptoms and signs. Babies will simply follow the definitions outlined above.

What could happen next. The biggest concern is that babies will stop breathing and not start again. In the absence of other untreated illnesses, this rarely happens. Most babies will resolve the problem on their own or with the help of medications to stimulate the breathing reflex.

What the doctor will do about it. First, she will look for a specific cause that can be reversed. She may draw blood from the baby to look for infection, low oxygen levels, and blood sugar or electrolyte problems. X-rays will look for infections or lung illnesses, and ultrasound may be used to look for intraventricular hemorrhage (see below). If the doctor has concern about your baby's brain development, she may order a CT scan or EEG (electroencephalogram).

If a cause cannot be found or cannot be reversed, your baby may be given oxygen, that same positive pressure support with the mask, or medication. Theophylline and caffeine both stimulate the nervous system and can encourage babies to breathe.

One side note here: If your babies had apnea, you may be bringing them home with monitors, called apnea and bradycardia monitors (A&B for short) until such time as the doctor feels comfortable with their ability to control their breathing on their own. Emma was put on one but didn't last long on it because her mom knew the evidence about them. The evidence has failed to show that babies are more likely to survive when put on these monitors, but it has also shown that parents of these babies suffer short- and long-term stress from the presence of this home version of the Machine, which will wake you at all hours of the night, terrified that your baby is dying, only to find out that a wire had come loose. Doctors sometimes recommend, and insurance gladly pays for, interventions that have little proven benefit but that make us feel better knowing we did *something* when little else could have been done. Talk to your doctor, always follow her advice, but be aware that the A&B monitor is not designed to save your baby from SIDS.

Jaundice

Definition. Jaundice is a yellowing of the skin produced by the presence of too much bilirubin in the body. Icterus is jaundice in the whites of the eyes. Bilirubin is a component of the red blood cells that helps them hold oxygen and is a product of the normal or abnormal breakdown of the red blood cells. Extreme jaundice can lead to kernicterus, which is the deposit of bilirubin in the brain tissue and can cause permanent brain damage. (There have also been a few reports of kernicterus in babies whose bilirubin level was not as high as we would have expected it to be.)

All jaundice is abnormal, but not all is dangerous. I will not be discussing what is called physiologic jaundice, which happens in normal newborns in the first week of life, or breast-milk jaundice, which happens later.

Causes and risk factors. Jaundice is caused when the body either makes too much bilirubin, is unable to process it well, or is unable to remove it from the body.

Risk factors include these:

1. A family history of jaundice
2. Prematurity
3. Polycythemia (too many red blood cells). This may happen with twin-twin transfusion syndrome (see chapter 14), gestational diabetes, pregnancy-induced hypertension, or a host of developmental problems including Down's syndrome.
4. Hemolytic anemia (blood cells being destroyed abnormally), which is seen with blood type incompatibility (Mom and baby have different blood types), the use of some medications, infection, or rare inherited blood diseases
5. Bleeding, particularly under the skin or in another place where it stays in the body and must be broken down into its parts, including bilirubin
6. Inherited liver or intestinal diseases, although these are rare

Symptoms and signs. Yellow skin is the first and major sign of jaundice. It often shows up first in the nose and face and spreads to the torso, arms, and legs. Although you may be told that the extent of jaundice does not predict the actual blood level of bilirubin, I know many nurses who could tell you spot-on every time—within two points—what a baby's level is based on their yellowing pattern.

What could happen next. The majority of cases of simple jaundice resolve with simple treatments. An underlying cause of the jaundice may cause problems of its own, but I will not describe all the possibilities here. If left untreated, severe jaundice can lead to permanent brain damage or death from kernicterus, that depositing of the pigment bilirubin in the brain.

What the doctor will do about it. The doctor will order blood tests to be done to determine the level of bilirubin in the baby's blood and other tests he deems prudent to look for a possible underlying cause. Mild cases are often followed using a wait-and-see approach, particularly in older babies. Sometimes all you may be told is to strip the baby naked and put him or her in a sunny window every day, because sunlight can help break the bilirubin in the skin into pieces that the body can remove through the kidneys. Underlying illnesses will be managed as needed.

Two medical treatments for jaundice are targeted either to helping the body process the bilirubin into a form the baby can remove from its system or to directly remove it. The first, using bili lights, utilizes the blue part of the rainbow to change that part of the bilirubin already in the skin into a form the baby can remove through its kidneys, since the liver is not yet fully capable of doing that job. This is the same as the "sunny window" approach used for less ill babies, but it removes bilirubin more reliably. The second treatment, called exchange transfusion, removes some of the baby's blood and replaces it with blood that has been cleaned of the excess bilirubin.

Intraventricular Hemorrhage (IVH)

Definition. IVH is a condition in which blood leaks into the brain. The source of bleeding is believed to be an area of poorly developed brain cells from which the brain forms and which disappears in most babies by the time they reach full term. There are four classes of IVH, depending on the extent of the bleeding, which are believed to correlate to the severity of the illness.

Causes and risk factors. IVH is caused when a baby is born while it still possesses this immature brain structure. Blood pressure changes associated with delivery or with normal changes in circulation that allow the baby to adapt to life outside its mother can cause rupture of the immature matrix and bleeding into the brain. Elevations in blood pressure from heart or lung problems can also cause IVH.

Risk factors include these:

1. Prematurity
2. Loss of baby's oxygen supply during labor
3. Hyaline membrane disease (HMD)
4. Pneumothorax (collapsed lung)

Symptoms and signs. The symptoms of IVH vary widely. Some babies have no problems at all, while others may have feeding problems, breathing problems, anemia, or seizures. In the worst cases, babies can experience coma, paralysis, or death.

What could happen next. A baby with IVH will have a prognosis that varies depending on how extensive the damage is. In the four-tier system of classifying IVH, those with Classes I and II have little to no difficulties at the age of five years compared with their peers. Those with Class III IVH have up to a 75 percent chance of developmental delay, varying from mild to severe. Babies who develop Class IV IVH have an almost 90 percent chance of death or of severe mental and physical handicap.

What the doctor will do about it. The doctor's best defense against IVH is the use of a preventative strategy. The ob-gyn will work hard to avoid the preterm delivery of your babies to reduce this risk. The neonatologist will do his best to avoid allowing wide variations in their blood pressures and will support their transition to the world outside your body. Despite intense investigation, we are at present left with few treatments once the IVH has happened.

Necrotizing Enterocolitis (NEC)

Definition. NEC is a disorder of premature infants in which the baby's immature intestines are attacked by toxins or by loss of blood flow. The addition of oral feeding provides the sugars needed for bacteria to grow, and the gases the bacteria produce invade the walls of the intestines. Eventually, parts of the intestines may die and begin to leak, causing infection and inflammation of the entire abdominal cavity.

Causes and risk factors. The specific toxins are as yet unknown. Risk factors for NEC include these:

1. Prematurity—the earlier the babies are born, the higher their risk for NEC
2. Low oxygen supply and heart failure
3. Receiving an exchange transfusion for jaundice

Symptoms and signs. In the first week to ten days of the baby's life, after feeding has started, he or she may have a distended belly, vomiting, bloody stool, or shock.

What could happen next. If left untreated, the baby could die from septic (infectious) or hypovolemic (low blood volume) shock. Like IVH, there is a staging system in place for NEC. Those with a more severe disease require more intensive therapy; those having NEC who develop perforation of the bowel have a 20 to 40 percent chance of death. Those who survive and are treated will catch up to their peers in growth, nutrition, and stomach function within the first year of life.

What the doctor will do about it. She will treat NEC very seriously. Babies with suspected or confirmed NEC are given nothing further by mouth until their condition stabilizes, and a tube will be inserted into their stomach to relieve pressure inside the intestines. The doctor will instruct the nurses to measure abdominal circumferences along with the other vital signs. She will do studies to look for signs of infection and will start them on antibiotics in their veins. She will monitor a baby with NEC closely and refer him or her for surgery if she feels it appropriate. If your baby does not need surgery, watch for when the doctor okays feeding the baby by mouth again, because it means she believes the baby is out of the woods to some extent.

Neonatal Sepsis

Definition. Sepsis is infection that has spread into the bloodstream. Neonatal sepsis is special because it affects only babies in the first month of life and because the causative bacteria are often different in newborns. It happens in one to ten per one thousand babies, which makes it among the more unlikely scenarios among all babies. However, because of its high mortality rate (13 to 50 percent) and because it attacks more preemies than full-term babies, it earns its spot on the list.

Causes and risk factors. Sepsis is caused when the baby comes in contact with bacteria, either from Mom or from others, which then finds its way into the bloodstream and tries to spread to other parts of the body.

Risk factors for neonatal sepsis include these:

1. Multiple pregnancy—great, we get our own risk factor!
2. Prematurity
3. Low birth weight at whatever gestational age
4. Prolonged rupture of membranes (Mom's water is broken), more than twenty-four hours prior to delivery
5. Fever in Mom before delivery
6. Babies who had fetal distress after birth
7. Babies who have had invasive tests or treatments (such as assisted breathing or intravenous lines)
8. Male sex
9. African-American background

Symptoms and signs. A baby with sepsis could have difficulty controlling her temperature, may develop changed behavior (irritable or lethargic where she once was not), and have feeding problems. She might also develop a rash, blue or mottled skin, and abnormalities of her heart rate and breathing.

What could happen next. As with any infectious illness, babies can be rapidly cured, slowly cured, linger with illness, or even die. It all depends on the cause of the illness, the strength of the baby to fight it, and the measures used to treat the baby.

What the doctor will do about it. In many cases the neonatologist will start antibiotics by IV even before she identifies a cause for the illness. This is because some illnesses develop and progress so quickly that she doesn't have time to see if she is correct. She will obtain the needed studies to find the cause and will then adjust her treatment accordingly. In cases where the baby has become weakened by the infection, she may need to put the baby on a ventilator to support breathing or prescribe fluids and/or medications to keep the blood volume high. New treatments involving immune system boosters instead of antibiotics as initial treatment may revolutionize the practice of medicine in this regard, but these treatments are not yet part of the standard of care in many areas.

The Feeder-Grower Newborn

Definition. Before your babies are discharged from the NICU, they will most likely have passed through this stage of life. What is called a "feeder-grower" in my region may be something else where you live, but the essence of the term is that it refers to those babies who are too young to have perfected the ability to assimilate sucking, swallowing, and breathing into a coordinated reflex to safely ingest food and are therefore supported by nursing staff—usually by being fed via a tube inserted through the nose or mouth into the stomach—until they are independent. Only when a baby can regulate his own temperature and eat and breathe safely can he go home with you (except in certain circumstances where it is expected your baby will always need help with one of these areas of life).

Causes and risk factors. Premature babies must mature enough to be able to coordinate the suck-swallow-breathe reflex so they can eat without food getting into their lungs, and they must have enough strength to avoid burning too many precious calories in order to gain benefit from their efforts. The reflex is believed to begin to mature sometime around thirty-four weeks of gestation. The strength depends on what other problems the baby has had to face that may have depleted his or her reserve energy.

Symptoms and signs. A feeder-grower may spit or cough while trying to take bottles or the breast. She may also require too much time to ingest the amount of food deemed necessary for her to sustain her growth and development.

What could happen next. If the situation goes untreated, the babies may aspirate food into their lungs, causing pneumonia. They may also expend so much energy eating that they are unable to grow appropriately. Rarely will any baby starve to death from this situation, but she could certainly have the types of trouble that come from malnutrition, including being underweight, having a weak immune system, or suffering developmental delay.

What the doctor will do about it. The doctor will order the nurses to monitor for this situation, and the nurses are quite skilled at doing so. If the baby should show signs of distress while eating or take too long to eat (and no illness is found that would be attributable to it), the nurses may insert a tube into the baby's stomach through which they will feed the baby until he matures enough to be able to do it on his own. You and their father will be encouraged to help feed the babies, as some babies do respond well to their parents' voices. This also provides necessary bonding time with each child and an opportunity for the nurses to teach you how to manage the feeding of preemies, which can be different from the feeding of fully grown babies.

Sixteen

Epilogue

The week I finished the final draft of this book, an amazing thing happened. One Saturday morning after breakfast, our now three-year-old twins ran upstairs, shut the door to the playroom, and told us not to bother them. For thirty minutes, Ben and I watched *Home & Garden Television* as Emma and Jack played "get the monster/oogie-boogie," "Sleeping Beauty and Prince Phillip," and "make a tent behind the sofa." We watched the sun rise over our cul-de-sac and illuminate the golden-leaved trees under clear skies, and we reveled in the silence. We *loved* it.

We had come upon a moment we had long been told to expect by those parents of twins who had taken pity on us and given us words of encouragement as we fed crying six-month-olds at the mall. It felt like our commencement, the end of our initiation into multiple parenthood. It was that glorious moment when the twins realized, for a short time at least, that they would rather be each others' playmates without interference from Mom or Dad. Other such moments are sure to follow, and having survived the initiation I feel ready to offer my services as a member of the next generation of sympathetic mothers of twins.

As you stand on the mesa peering at a seemingly blank desert plain, wondering what course your life will take from here, let me be the voice you hear in the wind telling you that you can take the plunge off the cliff and find that plain to be surprisingly rich and full of life once you get there. Despite the complications, the preterm labor, the hospital stays, the NICU, and those rough first months, having twins has been a marvelous experience, one I would never trade. Emma and Jack have become, like most multiples, healthy, happy, and whole children. They go to preschool and make friends. They sing songs in two languages. They play hard and require no special treatment.

Above all, our twins have a special bond that other children wish they could have with someone. They are best friends, playmates, confidantes, and accomplices—even as toddlers. They thoroughly enjoy telling people, "We're twins, and you're not," even when we try to encourage them to be nice. They know that they will always have each other, even when Mom and Dad are long gone. And Mom and Dad have the hope they will always remain as close as they are now.

If only those nay-saying parents of singletons could see us right at this moment. Far from our twins taking our lives away from us, they have enriched us beyond measure.

Parenthood of twins has changed me forever and for good, and it will change you, too. I no longer fret over insignificant problems, because I remember when things were much harder. I appreciate my husband even more than before (if that were possible) because of what we went through together and how he supported me. I appreciate my profession more, because I've seen what doctors could do for me and for my babies. I appreciate my patients more, both because they stuck by me through my inconvenient absences and because I know the pain many of them have suffered. I appreciate my job more, because I understand the unique opportunity I have to help someone else conquer fears and face illness. And, above all, I appreciate my God more, because I understand better now what true love is and what it does for others.

Long after you have passed through the trials of pregnancy with multiples, you will reflect on this experience and how it has shaped your life (if hormonal amnesia did not get a hold of you!). You will,

I hope, come away stronger than before, and ready to assume your position among the cognoscenti, ready to initiate the new member of the club when you see her navigating that double-wide stroller through the department store aisles. She will need a friend. You'll remember. You'll have been there.

Resources

American College of Obstetrics and Gynecology (ACOG)
www.acog.org

MOM Groups

From friendly advice to hand-me-downs, you need look no further than your local Mothers of Multiples (MOM) Groups for help. Most even hold regular meetings for away-from-home interaction with real-live adults, complete with babysitting!

NATIONAL ORGANIZATIONS AND SUPPORT GROUPS

National Organization of Mothers of Twins Clubs, Inc.
www.nomotc.org
P. O. Box 438
Thompsons Station, TN 37179-0438

Twins-Club.com: www.twins-club.com
Twinsclub UK: www.twinsclub.co.uk
Twins Magazine: www.twinsmagazine.com

U.S. State and Local Mothers of Multiples Organizations with Web Sites

This couldn't possibly be a complete list, but boy, did I try! I chose not to include clubs without Web sites because in some cases it meant publishing the personal e-mail addresses and/or telephone numbers of individuals who may or may not still be involved with the clubs.

ALABAMA

Birmingham area: www.bamom.org

Columbus area: www.webspawner.com/users/cmoms/index.html

Huntsville area: www.orgsites.com/al/hamom

ARIZONA

Arizona State Mothers of Multiples Organization: www.asmomo.org

East Tucson: www.geocities.com/easttucsonmothersofmultiples

Phoenix: www.geocities.com/Heartland/Cottage/7136

Tempe: www.dsmom.org/club_info.html

ARKANSAS

Little Rock: www.littlerockkids.com/parents/hobbies/twins.html

CALIFORNIA

Bakersfield: www.scmotc.org/ttcbakersfield.htm

Bay area, Northern California: www.mppom.org

El Dorado: www.edmoms.org

Elk Grove, Sacramento: awemoms.150m.com

Indio/Palm Springs: www.deserttwinmoms.org

Lancaster, Palmdale: www.multiplesupport.com

Marin: www.mpomc.org

Northern: www.ncamotc.homestead.com

Oakland: www.homestead.com/twinsbythebay/index.html

Orange County: www.multiplemiraclemoms.tripod.com

Pomona Valley: www.pvmotc.org/index.html

Sacramento: www.sacramentomothersofmultiples.org

San Diego (older multiples): www.members.aol.com/sdmumms

Santa Barbara: www.santabarbaramoms.org

Santa Clara County: www.sccmotc.com

Santa Cruz: www.geocities.com/Heartland/5000

Solano County: www.solanotwins.com

Southern: www.scmotc.org

South Orange County: www.smomc.org

Temecula Valley: www.scmotc.org/tvmom.htm

COLORADO

Denver: www.mothersofmultiples.com
Fort Collins: www.twinsntriplets.com
Westminster: www.darlingdoubles.org

DISTRICT OF COLUMBIA

www.triplicate.net

FLORIDA

Florida Organization of Mothers of Twins Clubs: www.flmotc.org
Bay area: www.bamoms.com
Broward County: www.pomwbc.freeservers.com
Dade County: www.miamimultiples.org
Jacksonville: www.jackpotts.org
Lakeland: www.angelfire.com/fl4/lakelandpoms
Orlando: www.gomott.org
Palm Beach County:
www.hometown.aol.com/wpbmotc/myhomepage/index.html
St. Petersburg: www.sppots.org
Sarasota: www.sarasotamultiples.com
Southwest Florida: www.homestead.com/swflpom/twins.html
Tampa: www.tampatwinsclub.org
Volusia County: www.geocities.com/volusiacountymomsofmultiples

GEORGIA

Atlanta: www.northmetromultiples.homestead.com
Cobb: www.cpomc.org
Columbus: www.webspawner.com/users/cmoms
www.noridetoolow.com/cmom
Fayette/Coweta Counties: www.smotc.tripod.com
North Fulton: www.nfmomc.org
South Fulton: www.thinkai.com/scmb

HAWAII

Oahu: www.amoms.homestead.com

IDAHO

Northwest: www.nwamotc.org

ILLINOIS

Illinois State Mothers of Twins Clubs, Inc.: www.iomotc.org
Chicago: www.geocities.com/Athens/Aegean/6929
Fox Valley: www.members.aol.com/dlmotc2/index.htm
McHenry: www.hometown.aol.com/mcmomsweblife/myhomepageprofile.html
North Chicago: www.twinsight.org
Schaumburg: www.oneplusonemoms.org
South Suburban: www.members.aol.com/deede2367/index.html
Springfield: www.spotc.twinstuff.com
Suburban Chicago:
www.palatinearea.info/multiplechoicemothersofmultiplesclub.html
West Suburban: www.geocities.com/wsmoms01/index.html
Will County: www.pages.ivillage.com/wcmotc

INDIANA

Indiana State Mothers of Twins Clubs: www.geocities.com/ifmotc
Indianapolis: www.geocities.com/southsidepom
Michiana: www.clix.to/mpomc
Northwest: www.groups.msn.com/MothersOfMultipleMiracles
Porter County: www.groups.msn.com/PorterCountyMothersofTwinsclub

IOWA

Des Moines: www.members.tripod.com/~DMMOM

KENTUCKY

Kentucky State Mothers of Multiples Club:
www.geocities.com/Heartland/Oaks/7557
Lexington: www.angelfire.com/ky/mtblan0/bpotmc.html
Louisville: www.louisvilletwinsclub.com

LOUISIANA

New Orleans: www.gnomotc.org

MARYLAND

Annapolis: www.annapolismoms.homestead.com/title.html
Columbia: www.camom.net

MASSACHUSETTS

Massachusetts State Mothers of Twins Association: www.mmota.org
New England: www.geocities.com/kpwmm
North Suburban: www.nspom.org
Worcester: www.worcester-motc.com/index.htm

MICHIGAN

Michigan Organization of Mothers of Twins Clubs, Inc.: www.momotc.org
Detroit: www.geocities.com/nws_mom
Greater Kalamazoo: www.gkmom.org
Grand Rapids: www.momotc.org/grmotc/index.htm
Huron Valley: www.comnet.org/hvmom
Lansing: www.geocities.com/Heartland/Estates/9261
Oakland County: www.gomoms.org
South Grand Rapids: www.geocities.com/momsclubgrsouth
Southwest Michigan: www.smmomc.twinstuff.com

MINNESOTA

Brainerd: www.geocities.com/brainerdmoms
Mankato: www.multipleblessings.50megs.com
Minneapolis: www.geocities.com/twintopics
St. Paul: www.stpaulmoms.org
Southern: www.geocities.com/mothersofmultiples

MISSOURI

Kansas City: www.gkcmotc.ourfamily.com
Lafayette: www.doublejoy.techgrafix.com
St. Louis: www.stlmotc.org
Springfield: www.multiplemoms.com

NEBRASKA

Lincoln: www.geocities.com/lincolnmultiplesclub
Omaha: www.opmc.home.att.net

NEVADA

Nevada State Mothers of Multiples Club: www.asmomo.org
Henderson: www.geocities.com/multiplesclub/momc.html
Las Vegas: www.lvmoms.com

NEW HAMPSHIRE

Nashua: www.geocities.com/Heartland/Pointe/3504

NEW JERSEY

Central: www.geocities.com/heartland/lane/5094
Edison: www.westfieldnj.com/mpmom
Hunterdon County: www.geocities.com/hcmom
Jersey Shore: www.maritimetwins.home.att.net
Middlesex/Monmouth: www.midjerseymoms.org
Raritan Valley: www.rvmom.org
Union County:
www.community.nj.com/cc/suburbanmothersoftwinsandtriplets

NEW MEXICO

Albuquerque: www.amotc.org

NEW YORK

New York State Organization of Mothers of Twins Clubs: www.nysomotc.org
Brentwood: www.mostonline.org
Buffalo: www.motcofbuffalo.com
Capital District (Albany): www.geocities.com/cdmotc1
Manhattan: www.manhattanmothersoftwins.org
Nassau: www.ncmotc.org
Rochester: www.grmotc.com
Rockland: www.rocklandmotc.homestead.com
Staten Island: www.community.silive.com/cc/simotc
Suburban Rochester: www.wsmotc.tripod.com/index.html
Suffolk County: www.motcsuffolkny.org

NORTH CAROLINA

North Carolina Mothers of Multiples: www.ncmom.org

OHIO

Ohio Federation of Mothers of Twins Clubs, Inc.: www.ofmotc.org
Canton: www.cantonmultiples.org
Columbus: www.cmotc.org
www.morethan1blessing.com
Dayton: www.daytontwinsclub.com

Emerald Valley: www.geocities.com/evmomc/index/html
Northeastern Cincinnati: www.nemotmc.freeservers.com
Southeast: www.semotc.org
Western Cincinnati: www.wcmotc.org
Westshore: www.wmotc.homestead.com

OKLAHOMA

Edmond: www.edmondmoms.com
Lawton: www.pages.prodigy.net/mbenner/lawtonftsilltwins.htm

OREGON

Northwest Association of Mothers of Twins Clubs: www.nwamotc.org

PENNSYLVANIA

Bucks/Montgomery: www.bucksmontmoms.org
Central PA: www.pages.ivillage.com/centralpapom
Chester County: www.ccmomc.org
Harrisburg: www.community.pennlive.com/cc/KMOM
Pittsburgh: www.npmoms.org
www.pmottq.twinstuff.com
www.shopmom.8m.com
Valley Forge: www.pages.ivillage.com/vfmottc

RHODE ISLAND

Blackstone: www.bvmotc.org

SOUTH CAROLINA

Palmetto State Parents of Multiples Club: www.members.aol.com/pspmsc
Aiken: www.members.aol.com/aikenmoms
Charleston: www.camom.org
Columbia: www.midnet.sc.edu/gcamotc
www.members.aol.com/PSPMSC/pt-moms.htm
Florence: www.pages.ivillage.com/twinmommie99/flomoms
Greenville: www.geocities.com/Heartland/Oaks/9903
Greenwood: www.greenwood.net/~gmotc
Sumter: www.members.aol.com/PSPMSC/sumtmom.htm

TENNESSEE

Clarksville: www.hometown.aol.com/clarksvilletwins/myhomepage/club.html
Knoxville: www.knoxtwinsclub.com
Memphis: www.memphistwins.org

TEXAS

Texas Mothers of Multiples: www.tmom.org
Abilene: www.angelfire.com/tx4/amom
Austin: www.austinmom.org
Beaumont: www.members.aol.com/gbmom
Beaumont/Southeast: www.setmot.org
Bellaire: www.bellairemoms.org
Brazos Valley: www.personalwebs.myriad.net/atouk/bvmotc
Dallas: www.dallastwins.org
Denton Area: www.damom.org
Fort Bend: www.fbpom.twinstuff.com
Garland: www.gamotc.org
Grapevine:
www.hometown.aol.com/lakecitytwinmom/myhomepage/club.html
Houston: www.spacecitytriplets.org
Houston/Galveston: www.geocities.com/Heartland/Hills/1637/index.html
Lubbock: www.lmom.org
Metrocrest: www.mpom.net
Mid Cities: www.mcmoms.org
New Braunfels: www.nbspom.twinstuff.com
North Dallas: www.ndmotc.org
Plano: www.pamom.org
Woodlands: www.wmoms.twinstuff.com

UTAH

Northern: www.multikids.org
Salt Lake: www.angelfire.com/ut/slmot
Utah Valley: www.pages.ivillage.com/uvmom

VIRGINIA

Alexandria: www.fcmom.org
Fredericksburg: www.famom.tripod.com
Loudoun/Fairfax: www.lfmomc.com
Portsmouth: www.hometown.aol.com/portstwins/myhomepageprofile.html
Tidewater: www.geocities.com/tmomc_99

WASHINGTON

Northwest Association of Mothers of Twins Clubs: www.nwamotc.org
Columbia Basin: www.basinbonusbabies.homestead.com/index.html
Seattle: www.orgsites.com/wa/nsfom
Spokane: www.miraclebonus.tripod.com
Tri-cities: www.cbvcp.com/twicenthrice

WISCONSIN

Wisconsin Organization of Mothers of Twins Clubs, Inc.: www.womotc.org
Madison: www.madisonmultiples.com
Waukesha: www.geocities.com/wmotc

Supplemental Insurer

Able to provide supplemental income in case of disability or illness, it can be an MOM's best friend.

AFLAC: www.AFLAC.com

Cool Stuff for Babies (and Infant Car Seats, Plus the Best Diaper Bags I Ever Found)

One Step Ahead: www.OneStepAhead.com
www.BabyTrilogy.com. My favorite cribs ever!
www.DoubleDeckerStroller.com. Strollers for twins & triplets.
www.morethan1.com. Strollers, nursing pillows, even stuff for quads and quints.
Twins Mall: www.twinsmagazine.com/twinsmall.html. From the editors of *Twins Magazine*
Ts for Two: www.tsfortwo.com. "I love my twin" peapod logo; too cute!
www.ToBuyTwo.com. The eBay for parents of multiples; buy, sell, or trade free.
www.Twice-as-nice-shop.com. Matching outfits for multiples.

Maternity Clothiers

From the inexpensive to the outrageous, here is everything you need to know to find clothes that you'll wear for just a few months and never want to see again. My favorites remain Target and Motherhood Maternity for their stylish selection at reasonable prices. Although you will be told to purchase the same size you wore before you were pregnant, I found I needed clothes up to two sizes bigger just to fit my ever-expanding abdomen!

I make no guarantees about the quality or service of the sites listed.

MATERNITY MASS-MARKET STORES

MaternityMall.com—the Web site for Motherhood Maternity

MimiMaternity.com

Babystyle.com—career casual and Pregnancy Survival Kit

OneHotMama.com—for those interested in showing a little skin even while bloated beyond recognition

AnnaCris.com—career and casual, some lingerie

Mothers-in-motion.com—exercise wear; endorsed by Cindy Crawford and Emme

BabyBecoming.com—plus size fashions

NicoleMaternity.com—chic fashions, including evening dresses and maternity wedding gowns

ApeaintthePod.com—on the upper end of retail chains but really nice stuff if you need it

Seraphine.com—casual wear from the United Kingdom

Embracefashion.com—for plus size moms

Avenue-des-bebes.com—French chic

MATERNITY VERSIONS OF FAVORITE CLOTHING LINES

OldNavy.com

LandsEnd.com

GapMaternity.com

Target.com—now features Liz Lange at a quarter of the price of her couture line

CUSTOM AND COUTURE MATERNITY (IN CASE YOU ARE INVITED TO THE WHITE HOUSE WHILE YOU'RE PREGNANT OR JUST FOR FUN IF YOU'RE NOT!)

Lizlange.com—the leader in maternity wear

VeroniqueMaternity.com—voted Best of New York 2003; this store carries casuals, dresses, business suits, and designers Diane von Furstenberg, Earl, and Chaiken as well as some Paris and Milan couture

Cadeaumaternity.com—European designs, both casual and formal

Carla-c.com—British design, nice formal and career wear ("the only hip alternative for future mums," according to *Elle* magazine)

Businessbump.co.uk—high-end business wear

Formes.com—French designs

Olianmaternity.com—casual and dress wear

Momstheword.com—trendy and funky casual, dress, and business wear

Support for Moms of Multiples

GENERAL SUPPORT

www.groups.yahoo.com/group/mothersofmultiples

multiples.about.com

multiples.about.com/mpchat.htm

familydoctor.org/handouts/170.html

SUPPORT FOR DADS

www.multiples.about.com/cs/dadsofmultiples

TWINLESS TWINS/INFANT DEATH

www.climb-support.org/enabled/index.html

www.twinlesstwins.org

Breast-feeding Resources

The Complete Book of Breastfeeding by Marvin S. Eiger, M.D., and Sally Wendkos Olds (New York: Workman, 1999).

Breastfeeding.com: www.breastfeeding.com

La Leche League, International: www.lalecheleague.org

American Academy of Pediatrics: www.aap.org

American Academy of Family Physicians (AAFP): www.aafp.org/afp/20010915/991ph.html

Nonpharmacologic Management of Labor Pain

Info from AAFP: www.aafp.org/afp/20030915/1109.html

Growing Families Newsletter:
www.library.osfsaintfrancis.org/agespecificnews/april2003/families.pdf

American College of Obstetricians and Gynecology (ACOG):
www.maternitywise.org/pdfs/laborpainexecsum.pdf

Pain Free Birthing: www.painfreebirthing.com

Child-Raising Resource (Newborns)

On Becoming Babywise: Learn How Over 500,000 Babies Were Trained to Sleep Through the Night the Natural Way by Gary Ezzo and Robert Bucknam, M.D. (Sisters, Ore.: Multnomah Books, 1998).

Social Security Disability

Provides supplemental income for parents of children with disabilities.

Social Security Administration: www.ssa.gov/disability

Includes listing of impairments that qualify:
www.ssa.gov/disability/professionals/bluebook/childhoodlistings.pdf

Nanny Resources

The Nanny Book: The Smart Parent's Guide to Hiring, Firing, and Every Sticky Situation in Between by Susan Carlton and Coco Myers (New York: St. Martin's Press, 1999).

The ABC's of Hiring a Nanny, Expanded Version, by Frances Anne Hernan (OLathe, Kans.: McGavick Field Publishers, 2000).

The Nanny and Domestic Help Legal Kit by J. Alexander Tanford and Brian A. P. Mooij (Vaperville, Ill.: Sphinx Publishing, 1999).

The Anxious Parents' Guide to Quality Childcare: An Informative, Step-by-Step Manual on Finding and Keeping the Finest Care for Your Child by Michelle Enrich (New York: Perigee Books, 1999).

Multiple Pregnancy Resources

When You're Expecting Twins, Triplets, or Quads: A Complete Resource by Barbara Luke (New York: Perennial Library, 2004).

Having Twins and More: A Parent's Guide to Multiple Pregnancy, Birth, and Early Childhood by Elizabeth Noble and Leo Sorger (Boston: Houghton Mifflin, 2003).

Index

About the Author

Rachel Franklin, M.D., is a board certified family medicine physician in practice with the Oklahoma City Clinic. Her special interest is in women's and children's health, and she practices obstetrics and pediatrics as part of her practice. Dr. Franklin is a frequent contributor to local media and volunteers her time as a teacher of family medicine at the University of Oklahoma College of Medicine. She also hosts a Web site, *www.AskDrRachel.com,* on which she posts informational articles in response to questions from visitors to the site.

Dr. Franklin is the proud mother of four-year-old twins, Emma and Jack, and wife to her husband, Ben. They live in Oklahoma City.